So

A great chronicle!

Pat Lamb

Then little children were brought to Jesus for him to place his hands on them and pray for them. But the disciples rebuked those who brought them.

Jesus said, "Let the little children come to me and do not hinder them, for the kingdom of heaven belongs to such as these."

(Matthew 19:13–14)

"Using her extensive experience in Christian education, Pat Lamb has created a twelve-month program of practical lessons for church and home. Bible verses are the basis, and direct communication with children for applying these principles will enlighten them on ways to react as they encounter life situations. No need to purchase supplies, since everyday materials are used to enhance these character-building sessions."

Ruth Fingado
Recipient of Exemplary Teaching Award
United States Department of Education

"Pat Lamb has written Let the Children Come from a heart of love for our Lord Jesus Christ and a passion for teaching children that the love of Jesus for little children is unsurpassed in human history. She has given her life to training children to come to Jesus, accept Him as Savior, and live for His glory, while trusting God to mean what He says in His Word that the child who receives training in the way of Christ 'will not depart from it.' Nothing is more important on this earth than to teach our children God's way and invite them to Jesus. Let the Children Come is a powerful tool in the hands of a caring pastor, teacher, parent, or grandparent who is devoted to using a few precious moments each week to instill God's truth in the hearts of our children. Your children will enjoy these brief lessons that will prepare them for living life abundantly with the full assurance they have given their hearts, souls, and minds to Jesus."

Morris H. Chapman
President and Chief Executive Officer
Executive Committee of the Southern Baptist Convention

Let the
Children
come

Pat Lamb

Let the Children come

TATE PUBLISHING & *Enterprises*

Let the Children Come
Copyright © 2009 by Pat Lamb. All rights reserved.

Scripture passages are taken from the New International Version (NIV) unless otherwise indicated. Some passages are taken from the King James Version and are indicated by (KJV)

Scripture quotations marked "NIV" are taken from the Holy Bible, New International Version ®, Copyright © 1973, 1978, 1984 by International Bible Society. Used by permission of Zondervan Publishing House. All rights reserved.

Scripture quotations marked "KJV" are taken from the Holy Bible, King James Version, Cambridge, 1769. Used by permission. All rights reserved.

The opinions expressed by the author are not necessarily those of Tate Publishing, LLC.

Published by Tate Publishing & Enterprises, LLC
127 E. Trade Center Terrace | Mustang, Oklahoma 73064 USA
1.888.361.9473 | www.tatepublishing.com

Tate Publishing is committed to excellence in the publishing industry. The company reflects the philosophy established by the founders, based on Psalm 68:11,
"The Lord gave the word and great was the company of those who published it."

Book design copyright © 2009 by Tate Publishing, LLC. All rights reserved.
Cover design by Janae Glass
Interior design by Travis Kimble & Lynly D. Grider

Published in the United States of America

ISBN: 978-1-60696-397-5
1. RELIGION / Christian Ministry / Children
09.03.27

Dedication

This book is dedicated to all children everywhere and to those who strive to help them grow in wisdom, stature, and favor with God and man.

Acknowledgments

The song "Without Him I Could Do Nothing" appropriately expresses my understanding of how this book and any other accomplishment in which I have been involved has happened. I am grateful to him for giving me my family who has been of great assistance in teaching me through the years. I appreciate the patience of our daughter, Trish, and our daughter-in-law, Kelly, in helping me learn more about the computer. Our son, David, has been a constant encouragement through his insistence that I write my feelings and thoughts. My husband, Keith, has been an encouragement through the years in my many endeavors. Our oldest and youngest sons, Kenneth and Charles, have been very supportive. Our grandchildren, Dylan, LeAndra, and Garrett, have served as my "laboratory" in recent years as I have tried many of my ideas on them.

Table of Contents

Introduction

Telling is not teaching. The Bible tells us to "Train up a child in the way he should go and when he is old he will not depart from it" (Proverbs 22:6). A child has not been trained until he acts out the teaching automatically.

It is a real challenge to teach children in such a way as to convince them that the right way is the best way. I once read, "We practice what we believe. All the rest is just religious talk." If we want children to act as God intended, we must get them to believe that way is preferable, not simply tell them that it is. As I have taught through the years, I have learned that all teaching should be geared to helping the child come to decisions on his own about right and wrong.

The lessons in this book are designed to help children think and decide in their own minds that God's way is best. Questions are used often to challenge the thought processes. Objects are used to form mental pictures. Emphasis is placed on developing understanding. Because so many people have become desensitized to pain and hurt around us, an attempt is made to stimulate feelings of compassion.

Most of the lessons take a minimum of preparation. However, let's not forget the value of what we are doing. Let's prepare adequately. To hurry and get something ready is to minimize the value of what we are doing. Programs on the computer make preparation easy. The Scripture verses can easily be printed. I have found that the children love to receive them on sticker paper or in the form of magnets. Pictures can also be obtained through computer programs. The Internet provides more than we will ever need in history or pictures.

What an opportunity to have children in our hands a few moments! Let's make those moments really count! Many churches, particularly smaller churches that do not have a sufficient number of children's workers, ask children to come to the front of the church at the beginning of the regular worship service. Some churches do this because they feel that children need to learn to stay in "big church" and this time makes it more interesting to them. Other churches use a time in front of big church to give the pastor an opportunity to work with the children.

When I personally did this worship time with children, I found that there were not many materials available for such presentations. It was with this thought in mind that I originally started writing this book. As the writing progressed, however, I realized that the lessons could easily be adapted for use in many situations. They could be used for the special worship often provided for children who are bussed to church, by parents or grandparents at home, or even in Sunday school. Although most denominations have their own Sunday school materials, these lessons could be used to supplement or fill in when particular emphasis is needed.

When these lessons are used during the regular worship service in front of the congregation, let's remember that the adults are listening. I have been amazed to see the growth in the adults who have listened to these lessons. Oftentimes they seem to comprehend what they have never understood before, or it may remind them of what they have forgotten. We are really teaching them, too.

These lessons take approximately five to ten minutes. However, much depends upon the person delivering the lesson. I would suggest that one use self-discipline to prevent rambling and stick to the topic. A good teaching procedure is to emphasize and reinforce one lesson at a time. Otherwise, the point is lost in confusion with everything else that is said. We find that it is difficult to hold the attention of children longer than five to ten minutes in front of the congregation. If need be, some lessons may be divided and used on two occasions rather than hold the children too long. They are intentionally designed to allow the teacher to pick and choose those parts appropriate in his or her situation. I have tried to include an ample amount of ideas so the deliverer will feel secure in knowing he or she has plenty to fill the time slot allowed.

Lessons have been designed for differing age levels since ages 12 and under usually will come to the front of the church when the pastor asks children to come forward for their special time. Most churches, even very small churches, will have nursery provided for age two and under. However, in my experience, some parents may even bring their toddlers up to the front and sit with them to begin teaching them to listen. It is the prerogative of the presenter to choose the activities and suggestions most appropriate for the particular group. I have tried to include both simple and more difficult activities to provide a choice. The lessons can be viewed as a smorgasbord from which to choose to meet the needs of the children present. In some cases, the older children can do activities and the younger children present can simply observe.

The New International Version of the Bible has been used in most cases. In some cases, the King James Version seemed more appropriate. It is necessary to take time to explain "shew," "hath," "thee," and "thou," as well as other words uncommon to our everyday usage if the King James Version is used.

Some of the most effective lessons for children are impromptu lessons. Parents might use these lessons at home as they seek to find teachable moments with their children and their children's friends. I can remember when our children were young, I would often look out in the yard and count as many as ten children. It was at such a time that I decided to do backyard Bible club. When children get together, they sometimes don't know what to play. Parents could intervene at a time like this and informally present one of the lessons outlined. Neighborhood story times are a conduit of God's love to the community.

Grandparents often find themselves wondering what to do with the grandkids when they come to visit. Having this book handy to flip open and find an idea can be a valuable use of the time.

A pastor, educational director, Sunday school teacher, and many others will find it helpful to use a lesson on occasion from this book to emphasize a point to fit an immediate need.

As I send this book to the publisher, it is my prayer that it be helpful in drawing folks nearer to Christ. Let's make every minute count! Let's remember Ephesians 5:16: "...making the most of every opportunity, because the days are evil."

January

It is only natural to think of setting goals during a time when making New Year's resolutions is talked about incessantly. As children hear others talk about making resolutions and in almost the same breath laughing about breaking those same resolutions, they can learn the fact that God is there to help them make—not promises—but realistic goals that can be accomplished with God's help. They also learn that God will forgive them if they make a mistake, and they need not give up but simply keep trying.

This month's lessons are based on Luke 2:52. The first Sunday deals with goal-setting in general. The following lessons take each of the four categories to deal with individually. Lessons deal with growth in wisdom, stature, favor with God, and favor with men.

"And Jesus grew in wisdom, and stature, and favor with God and men" (Luke 2:52).

Go Where?

Scripture verse: "Without a vision, the people perish." (Proverbs 29:18, KJV)

Materials needed:

• Printed copies of memory verse.

• Printed flash cards or slips of paper with the words "vision" and "perish"

• Chart tablet or other writing surface such as a dry board or chalk board

• A piece of spoiled fruit such as a brown banana

Procedure: Ask one child to stand up and obey you when you tell him/her what to do. When the child is standing, say "go," but do not tell the child where to go. The expected response is for the child to ask, "Where?" Repeat the word "go." Point out that it is impossible to go somewhere unless we know where we are going.

Talk about the importance of setting goals, and compare goals in life to the example just given. Explain that if we do not set goals, we flounder around and achieve very little or nothing. Using the chart tablet, ask the children to list either short-term or long-term goals that they may have. Include such goals as to learn all we can learn in school and church, obey parents and teachers, respect others, do kind deeds, etc. (An older child may be used to do the writing.)

Using one of the goals listed, use another page of the

chart to ask the children to list ways this goal can be accomplished. Children have a tendency to use general terms. It is important that children ages 6 and above learn to be specific. For example, if the goal of learning is used, list such things as doing homework, listening carefully to instructions from the teacher, using what is learned at school or home and other places, trying hard to remember, reading, writing down what is learned, repeating what is learned, etc.

As time permits, do the same with the other goals listed leading children to see that we do not achieve goals without doing specific actions.

Introduce the memory verse: Hand out copies of the memory verse. Show the flash cards of the words "perish" and "vision." Show the piece of spoiled fruit. Explain that the meaning of the word "perish" means to spoil and that "vision" means a picture in our minds. Setting goals means having a picture in our minds of where we want to go. Ask the children to close their eyes and see if they can see a picture in their minds of a goal they would like to achieve.

Repeat the memory verse several times.

OOOOO

Prayer: Dear Jesus, please help us to know what goals to set that would be pleasing to you. Please help us to remember our goals and to work hard to achieve them. Amen.

Parent tip: Take time during the coming week to sit down with the child and write out his/her goals. Post the list in a prominent place and remind the child often of what has been written. Be sure to help the child to know what is necessary in order to achieve the goals.

Note: This lesson may be done without taking the added time to talk about how to achieve the goals and simply save that part for future lessons.

Growing Like Jesus

Scripture verse: "And Jesus grew in wisdom and stature, and in favor with God and men." (Luke 2:52)

Materials needed:

• Flannel board with words "mental," "physical," "spiritual," and "social" on strips of paper or a writing surface where these words can be written such as a dry board or chalkboard.

• Paper and pencil for each child

• Copies of today's Scripture verse for children to take home

---

Procedure: Talk to the children about the importance of setting goals. Read the verse: "Where there is no vision, the people perish" (Proverbs 29:18).

Read today's memory verse. Ask the children to name the four areas of growth mentioned. Tell the children that wisdom is associated with mental growth, stature is associated with physical growth, favor with God is associated with spiritual growth, and favor with men is associated with social growth.

Show the four strips of paper with the words social, mental, physical, and spiritual. Place them on the flannel board. Tell the children that God wants us to grow in all four areas as Jesus did, but that sometimes people neglect some areas and just grow in other areas. To be well balanced, we need to grow in all areas.

Place the strips in a square on the flannel board. Point out that if we grow equally in all areas, the square represents us. Now tear off or fold back the strip that says "spiritual." Show the geometric design by pulling two strips to meet the spiritual strip to illustrate that now the square is gone.

Continue showing different designs by altering the size of the strips to illustrate that people grow in different ways.

Give each child a pencil and paper. Ask the children to draw a long line if they feel they are really good at making friends. Tell them to label it "social." Ask each child to draw a short or long line to show if they are growing strong and are healthy and to label it "physical." Repeat this procedure for "mental," asking them to draw a line to show if they make good grades in school and like to learn. Finally, ask the children to draw a line to show how they feel they have grown in learning about Jesus and to label it "spiritual." Ask the children to connect the lines. Tell them that this may show them the areas where they need to try harder to grow. (You may want to enlist adults to help with this.) (If this lesson is being done at home with children who are not yet able to write, an adult may simply draw a square and label it with the four areas. Then, the adult may simply tell the child that we need to try to grow equally in all four areas and that you, as an adult will help them to do so.)

Note: If preferred, strips of paper of various lengths may be prepared ahead of time for the children to choose and arrange. This may be easier than having the child draw the design. The strips could be arranged on the floor or bench if at the front of the church.

OOOOO

Discuss with the children where they think they need to grow the most. Suggest that the children set goals to grow in that area. As time permits, suggest goals according to the areas the children mentioned and ways to achieve those goals.

Prayer: Father, help us to grow socially, mentally, physically, and spiritually just like Jesus did. Help us to set goals for each of these areas to make sure that we please Jesus. Amen

Parent tip: Discuss with your child his/her strengths and weaknesses. Review goals from last week to ensure that goals are set for improvement in areas needed. You may want to redo the drawing that represents the child's growth while there is more time to discuss each area.

Pleasing Jesus
by Learning His Word

Scripture verse: "Do your best to present yourself to God as one approved." (2 Timothy 2:15)

Materials needed:

• Copies of verses from this and previous lessons made into a necklace by stringing on yarn with beads in between each verse

• Chart from previous lesson on setting goals showing that one goal for the new year is to memorize Scripture

Procedure: Show the chart where goals for the new year were listed and point out that one of the goals that the children named was to memorize Scripture. Mention that one way to grow spiritually is to read the Bible and memorize Scripture. Ask if any of the children would like to say a verse that he or she has memorized and allow the child to do so.

Tell the children that when Jesus was a child he, too, memorized Scripture. He had to go to school and learn about the things in the Bible. Although the New Testament was not available at that time, the Old Testament was available. Children in Jesus' time studied the Old Testament. It would be good to show the divisions in a real Bible. Also, tell the children that God has said that we should write Scripture on the "tablet of our hearts" and explain that there is no real tablet, but that he meant that we should memorize Scripture.

Show one of the necklaces and go over each verse reminding children of the meaning of each verse. Suggest that the children say each verse one or two times at each mealtime. By doing so, they will soon know the verse. Go over ways of memorizing Scripture, such as writing down a part of the verse and saying it over and over. Explain that the verse may be put on the bathroom mirror so it can be seen when they brush their teeth. Allow the children to share other ways they may learn the Scripture. Put a necklace on each child.

○○○○○

Prayer: Thank you, Father, for your word in the Bible. Help us to memorize your word so we will always remember how to please you. Amen

Parent tip: Place a copy of the Scripture verse on the dining table and ask the child to read or say it at each meal. Assist the child in memorization by asking for a recitation of the verse often. Don't forget to give praise for accomplishments.

Children Need to Obey Parents

Note: This is a more difficult lesson than one might readily recognize. In today's world, many children are abused and expected to obey parents in things that are decidedly wrong. We can no longer tell children to obey parents in all circumstances. Yet, children need to learn to be respectful to parents. We must understand that it is not an easy thing for children of parents who do not know the Lord to follow this commandment.

Scripture: "Children obey your parents in the Lord, for this is right." (Ephesians 6:1)

Materials needed:

• Two objects, such as yardsticks, to use for starting and stopping bases in the game, "Mother, May I"

• Printed Scripture cards of verse to memorize

Discussion: Ask the children if it is ever hard for them to obey their parents. Discuss the reasons for obeying. This would include points such as safety, learning right from wrong, and the fact that we are commanded to obey in the Scripture.

What does it mean to obey? To obey means to do what we are told to do. Because our parents are more experienced, they usually know what is best. However, even parents can make mistakes.

When we are asked to do something we know is wrong or that we can't do, we should still respect our parents and tell them nicely how we feel about the situation. We can say, "I would like to obey you, but I can't do that right now" or "I would like to obey you, but Jesus says we should not do that."

Game: "Mother, May I"

Ask a couple of adults from the congregation to assist with this game and allow the children to participate as is appropriate. The adults will catch on faster and make the game go more smoothly. Otherwise, a lot of the congregation's time will be wasted. The game needs only to be done for a few moments to give the children the idea of obedience. (This game can easily be played at home with only two players and a person to give instructions. Children seem to really like this game.)

Place a starting and stopping base in place. Have the players line up at the starting base. The presenter acts as "mother." The presenter tells one person, "Carol, take two giant steps." Each player must say "Mother, may I" before proceeding. If the player forgets, he or she must go back to the starting base.

Other commands include scissor steps (steps are taken by crossing legs), backward steps, baby steps, or normal steps. The object is to get to the other base first.

This game teaches listening skills, memory recall, and manners as well as obedience. Parents and children may be inclined to pursue the playing of the game more at home, thus providing a good parent-child activity.

Scripture verse: Hand out the Scripture cards and ask the children to repeat the verse several times.

OOOOO

Prayer: Have a circle of prayer. Father, help us to be willing to obey our parents, our teachers, and others who have authority over us. Amen

Parent tip: Take time during the coming week to play this game with your child and his/her friends. Assist the child in memorizing the Scripture verse.

February

February, the month of love, is a good time to emphasize our relationships to others. We need to help the children have a clear definition of the word "love." They need to understand the difference in loving a hamburger, for instance, and loving people as described in 1 Corinthians 13. Perhaps the following lessons will help to accomplish this goal.

Being Considerate

Scripture verse: "In everything, do to others what you would have them do to you, for this sums up the Law and the Prophets." (Matthew 7:12)

Materials needed:
_____

• Two flat plates

• Two tall, narrow vases

• Two pretty napkins or a table runner

• Picture of a fox

• Picture of a crane

• Printed copies of the Scripture verse
_____

Procedure: Show the picture of the fox, and ask the children how we usually describe a fox (sly, sneaky, deceitful, likes to eat chickens, etc.). Then show the picture of the crane and have the children describe what they know about a crane.

If children say that cranes bring babies, simply tell the children that sometimes we see pictures showing a crane carrying a baby but that is just a kind of joke. Cranes do not really bring babies. (Most children in today's world, even at a very young age, know that babies are in ladies' tummies.) If the conversation turns too complicated to discuss at this time, simply tell the children that their mommies and daddies can explain to them where babies come from.

Tell the following story after explaining to the children

the meaning of a fable. A fable is a story that is not really true but teaches us a truth about behavior. While telling the story, set the table with the plates for the first part of the story; then, remove the plates, and place the vases in place for the second part.

Fox and the Crane

Once upon a time, a sly old fox invited a crane to have dinner with him. He may have really wanted to eat the crane but thought he would have a little fun with him first. The crane accepted the invitation and on a certain day arrived at the fox's home. The fox proceeded to set the table with a pretty cloth and a plate for each. The fox poured milk in the plates and quickly lapped up the milk on his own plate.

The crane looked at the plate and realized that the fox had played a trick on him because there was no way the crane could drink the milk from the flat plate with his long beak.

Suspecting that the fox really wanted to have him for dinner, he thought very fast and quickly said, "Please, Mr. Fox, do me the honor of coming to my home for dinner so that I may return your favor to me."

Thinking that he would get another dinner before eating the crane, the fox gladly accepted the invitation.

On the day appointed, the fox arrived at the crane's home for dinner to find that the crane had set the table with two tall vases. As the crane proceeded to dine from the tall vase, the fox realized that he could not get his tongue deep enough into the vase to get the food. He became angry and decided to eat the crane. However, the crane knew what he was thinking and quickly flew up out of the reach of the fox.

Hopefully, the fox learned a lesson. He should have treated the crane as he wanted to be treated.

Discuss with the children how the fox did not consider the needs of the crane. Ask the children if they sometimes forget to consider the needs of people around them and explain that each person is different and has unique needs and desires.

Introduce the Bible verse: Pass out copies of today's Bible verse, and have the children repeat it several times. Tell them that this verse if called the "golden rule" because it is so important.

OOOOO

Prayer: Dear Jesus, help us to think of others more than ourselves. Please help us to understand the needs and wants of people around us. Please help us to remember to treat others as we want to be treated. Forgive us for the times when we have been selfish. Amen

Parent tip: Look for ways the child is showing consideration to others during the week and give praise for doing so. Plan a family project that shows consideration for a neighbor such as taking a dish to a sick person.

"I'm Sorry"

Scripture verse: "But unless you repent, you too will all perish." (Luke 13:3)

Materials needed:

• Printed Scripture verses for children to take home

• Small slips of paper and a pencil for each child

• A large container such as a large pot or pan

• Matches or lighter

• Candle in holder

• Aluminum foil

• Barbeque or salad tongs

Preparation: Place aluminum foil in the bottom of the pan for protection. Place the candle, in a sturdy holder, in the center of the pan. Have the pencils sharpened and the paper ready.

Procedure: Ask the children to name four things everyone should learn to say often. They are "I'm sorry," "excuse me," "please," and "thank you." Tell the children that today you will talk about saying, "I'm sorry."

Ask the children if they know of someone who will quickly say they are sorry and not mean it. Ask them if they know someone who will never say they are sorry. Tell the children that we should say that we are sorry but that we should really mean it whenever it is said.

Give each child a slip of paper and a pencil. Ask the children to write down one thing that they have done wrong for which they are sorry. (Younger children may draw pictures.) Make sure the children know that no one will read what is written. It is just between the child and God. When the children finish, ask them to bow their heads and tell God that they are sorry and ask for his forgiveness.

After the children have prayed, ask them to come and bring their slips of paper. Using tongs, assist the children in burning the slips of paper. Explain that when God forgives us, the sin is gone and he removes it as far as the east is from the west. However, sin has natural consequences. Even though God forgives us, some things are hurtful to others and ourselves, and we still have to deal with the consequences. Give examples such as drug use, use of alcohol, etc. God, however, will not hold it against us.

Scripture verse: Pass out the printed verse and discuss its meaning in connection with the exercise done today. Ask the children to repeat the verse a few times.

Note: If you have a very large group of children, choose four or five to do the exercise and the others can observe.

OOOOO

Prayer: Father, help us to be careful and do things to help, and not hurt, others. I am sorry for the times I have done things that have been hurtful to others. Help me to remember to say "I'm sorry," and really mean it, when I do something to others that I should not do. Amen

Parent tip: Be sure to say "I'm sorry" yourself whenever you do something wrong in order to set a good example for the children. It is good to say you are sorry to your child when warranted.

"Please"

Scripture verse: "In everything, do to others what you would have them do to you." (Matthew 7:12)

Materials needed:

• Printed Scripture verses for children to take home

Procedure: Remind the children that there are four things that everyone should be able to say often. We should all say "excuse me," "I'm sorry," "please," and "thank you." In this lesson, we will practice saying "please."

Play a game: Ask the children to line up horizontally at one side. Tell them that they are to take turns asking, "May I take a step, please?" If they take a step without asking, they have to go back one step. The object is to see who gets to the finish line first. (Note: Ribbons may be used on carpet to mark lines or simply point out locations.)

Tell them that you will not be prompting them but that they are to remember by themselves. After doing this for a few minutes, ask the children to sit down. Remind them that when we try to learn something, we should do it seven times to make it begin to stick. Ask if they think they can remember to say please. (Even though this game is similar to "Mother, May I" that was used in a previous lesson, it is still good to do it. It serves as a reinforcement of the original learning and a reminder to say "please.")

Discuss appropriate times to say please. Talk about being considerate of others and explain that having good manners and saying please is one way to show kindness to others.

Introduce the Scripture verse: Ask the children to say it several times. Explain the meaning of the verse and why it is called "the golden rule." Encourage the children to memorize the verse and to try to live by this rule for the remainder of their lives.

OOOOO

Prayer: Father, please help us to remember to say "please." Amen

Parent tip: Remember to say "please" when talking with your children. Refrain from giving orders. Treat children as though they are "little grown-ups" whenever possible. Of course, there are times when the parent must tell the child to do something whether that child wants to do it or not. The parent is the authority, not the child.

"Excuse Me"

Scripture verse: "But be ye doers of the word and not hearers only." (James 1:22, KJV)

Materials needed:

- Chart tablet and colored markers

- Printed copies of today's Bible verse to give to the children

Procedure: Explain to the children that it is good that they come to Sunday school and church and that it is important that they listen carefully to learn what the Bible instructs us to do.

Today's Bible verse tells us that it is even more important to be doers of what the Bible tells us and not just hearers.

Read the Bible verse and hand out the copies to the children. Ask them to read the verse together a few times. Allow children to choose a favorite color of marker. Allow the children, one at a time, to write a word of the Bible verse on the chart tablet. Assist the children as necessary. Occasionally repeat the verse as the children write the words. When the verse is completed, ask the children to repeat the verse again. Then ask for volunteers to say the verse alone.

Discuss examples of ways to be doers and not just hearers of God's word. Explain that when we do things that might inconvenience others, we should say "excuse me." By doing so, we are a doer of being kind and considerate of others.

Role-play situations where saying "excuse me" would be appropriate. One example would be when adults are talking and children need to go between them to get to where they are going. Another example might be stepping on someone's toe. The children will assuredly think of other situations.

Stay close by, telling the children that you will be watching to see who remembers to say "excuse me."

Introduce the Scripture verse. Review the meaning of the verse and have the children repeat it again.

OOOOO

Prayer: Father, help us to do the things we should and not just listen to lessons and then forget them. Please help us to remember to say "excuse me, please" when we should. Thank you for people who practice good manners. Amen

Parent tip: Don't forget to say "excuse me" to your children often.

March

I once saw a sign on the door of a kindergarten classroom that read, "Children are people, too." We sometimes forget that children have very real problems.

This month's lessons deal with common problems that children face that may become hindrances to their decisions to please Jesus. We often tell children to be good but don't give them tools to know how to deal with their problems. This series of lessons will hopefully help the children identify and deal with common bumps in their road of life.

Bumps in the Road of Life

Note: This is the first in a series of lessons with this theme.

Scripture verse: "For the Lord your God is the one who goes with you to fight for you against your enemies to give you victory." (Deuteronomy 20:4)

Materials needed:

• Printed copies of the Scripture verse to hand out

• Banner with the words: "Road of Life"

• Piece of fabric or paper long and narrow to put out to resemble a road

• A doll, cutout of a child, toy car, or truck to go along the road

• A few rocks about four or five inches in diameter

• Small signs that say:

  • Someone told a lie about me.

  • My friend told my secret after promising not to tell.

  • I got blamed for something I didn't do.

  • I have to do something I don't like to do.

  • Sometimes I feel like no one likes me.

  • I don't like to sit still.

- I get bored.

- My clothes, car, and home are not as good as those of my friends.

- Sometimes my relatives embarrass me.

- Sometimes I just want to sleep and not go to church.

- Someone yelled at me.

Procedure: Lay out the fabric or paper making a road. Place the rocks along the road and the car, truck, doll, or person at the beginning of the road. Place the banner beside the road.

Ask the children how many of them really try to be good. Ask them if sometimes things happen that seem hard to deal with and they sometimes forget to be good and perhaps get angry or disobey.

Explain that when we are born, we begin a journey on the road of life and many times things happen that seem like bumps in that road. Ask the children to tell what things make it difficult for them to be good and please Jesus as they go through each day.

Give the children an opportunity to discuss some of the things they find difficult to deal with. Then show the signs with the things listed above. Mention each briefly, and ask if they have ever had to face any of these things. Let the children know that during the next few weeks, there will be lessons to help them know what Jesus says to do when they face some of these things.

Read the Scripture verse. Tell the children that we all need to remember that God is always with us to help us overcome any battle we must face. The bumps in the road are like battles, and God will help us have victory over these obstacles. Ask the children to repeat the verse with you.

○○○○○

Prayer: Dear Father, help us remember that you see everything and that you are always near us. We know that you are the best and strongest of all and you can win our battles for us. Amen

Parent tip: During the week, watch your child and take note of the things that seem to upset him or her. Take time to sit down and discuss why he or she is upset and to give suggestions as to how to deal with the situation. Let those who work with your child know what seems to be upsetting him/her so that future lessons might be prepared on this subject.

Someone Lied about Me

Scripture verse: "Love your enemies and pray for those who persecute you." (Matthew 5:44)

Materials needed:

• Use the road, banner, and signs from the previous week's lesson. Use only one rock to represent the "bump in the road" when someone lies about us.

• Printed copies of the Scripture verse

Procedure: Review the lesson from last week. Introduce the topic for today that had been mentioned in the discussion of "bumps in the road." Place one rock on the road and using the object selected to travel the road, move it along the road to the rock, indicating that it has reached an obstacle. As you discuss dealing with the obstacle, move the rock out of the way.

Allow the children to discuss a time they remember when someone told a lie about them or when they were blamed for something they did not do. Discuss the feelings involved in both the child who was lied about and the person doing the lying.

Help the children understand that even the person who did wrong felt badly, too. Discuss reasons the person may have lied such as fear of getting in trouble, jealousy, or thoughtlessness.

Read Matthew 5:43–48 to the children. Discuss the Scripture. Ask the children if they find it hard to pray for someone who has done something wrong to them. Help them to understand that God loves everyone and will forgive when we repent and ask for forgiveness. Explain that God removes our sins as far as the east is from the west and that east and west never touch.

Suggest that if the situation happens again where someone lies about them, to simply stay calm and wait for God to deal with the situation. Remind the children that it is always best to tell the truth, and we should feel sorry for the person who is doing wrong. We need to help others learn about Jesus in a kind and loving way. God will always see to it that justice is done, but it may not happen as quickly as we would like.

We really should not want bad things to happen to anyone no matter how badly they treat us. It is best for them to learn God's way.

Read the Scripture verse together. Remind the children that they may not always have the opportunity to learn Scripture and they should try very hard to memorize as much Scripture as possible.

OOOOO

Prayer: Father, help us have good minds so we can remember Bible verses. Thank you for your Bible that tells us how to act. Amen

Parent tip: Watch for an instance during the week when the child feels he is being treated unfairly. Sit down and talk with the child about why the other person may have acted as he or she did. This will help develop compassion and understanding as well as helping the child to deal with tough situations.

Someone Yelled at Me

Scripture verse: "A gentle answer turns away wrath, but a harsh word stirs up anger." (Proverbs 15:1)

Materials needed:

• Rocks, road, and little truck from previous two lessons

• A picture of an angry person yelling

• A dollar bill

• Copies of today's Bible verse

Procedure: Place the rock on the road from last week's lesson with the labels: "Someone lied about me" and "Someone blamed me for something I didn't do." Ask the children to tell what they remember from the previous two weeks' lessons. Allow someone to quote the memory verses from those lessons and remind the children that God is always fair even when people aren't.

Remind the children that two weeks ago, one of the items listed that is a bump in the road of life was being upset when yelled at. Now place another rock on the road with the sign, "Someone yelled at me."

Say, "As we travel along the road trying to serve Jesus, sometimes we get yelled at and it bothers us."

Ask the children to tell you how they feel when someone yells at them and why it bothers them. Bring out such words as frustrating, hurt, guilty, ashamed, unloved, angry, bitter, and embarrassed. Ask the children if they ever feel like yelling back, or if they sometimes feel like they would like to get even. Spend some time discussing these feelings.

Now, ask the children if they have ever gotten angry and yelled at someone else. Ask them to describe how they think that person felt. Help the children to see that they caused the same feelings in others that they, themselves, have felt.

Give the children the opportunity to explain why they yelled and ask them if it accomplished any good thing. Tell the children that we should choose actions to accomplish good things. If we want someone to behave in a different manner, yelling is not the best way to go about it.

Allow those who would like to give ideas as to what they should do when someone yells at them. Suggest that they say, "I'm sorry," and walk away as one thing they could do. Help them to understand that many times people yell because they don't know what else to do.

Explain the word "persuasion." Give an example. Give a dollar bill to a child. Tell another child to try to get the first child to give him the dollar. As he proceeds, point out the methods being used. He may yell at him, coax him, persuade him, etc. Discuss which ways worked best and give suggestions as to what the child could have done.

Introduce the Bible verse. Tell the children that the Bible gives us instructions for getting along with other people. Read today's verse with the children. Tell them that they should not yell at others in an angry manner because it just makes the other person angry. Repeat the verse several times.

OOOOO

Prayer: Dear Father, Help us to be kind to others and to

remember not to yell at anyone. Please show me ways to talk to people in a nice way. Help us to have the love in our hearts as we should for others. Amen

Parent tip: When children misbehave, take the time to explain a better way of acting to them. Best of all, plan ahead and avoid incidents rather than waiting until they happen and then becoming frustrated about them. Remind them of Ephesians 6:4 where we are told not to provoke children to wrath. Also, remind them that children learn by example. They will mimic the yelling they receive by yelling at pets, other children, etc.

Everybody Has Better Things than Me

Scripture verse: "Man looks at the outward appearance but the Lord looks at the heart." (I Samuel 16:7)

Materials needed:

• Rocks, road, small truck, and signs from previous three lessons

• Copies of today's verse for children to take home

• Dressed-up Barbie doll and Barbie doll clothes

Procedure: Review highlights from the past three lessons while placing the rocks on the road with the signs. Add a sign for today with today's title on it.

Introduce today's lesson by asking the children if they ever think that the things they have are not as nice as what other people have. Provide an opportunity for children to tell some of the things they would like to have. Also, take a few moments to name some of the things that are nice to have in the home. Items might include a plasma TV, new appliances, stereo systems, etc.

Show the Barbie doll and her clothes. Ask the girls if they ever thought they would like to grow up and have pretty things like Barbie. Then ask if they know anyone grown up who really looks like Barbie. Help them to see that most people do not really look like Barbie. Point out that toys, TV, billboards, magazines, etc., often stimulate us to want to have more and more. (You may want to also use a GI Joe doll or Ken as an example for the boys.)

Inform those present that many people in other countries do not even have a house to live in. Some people in South America live in cardboard shelters on the hillsides or in huts with dirt floors. Other examples may be given as come to mind. (It would be even more effective to show pictures of children in other lands in poverty if those are available.)

Ask the children to tell you things they have that they could do without. Help them to see the difference between needs and wants.

Now introduce the verse for today. Read it aloud in unison several times. Remind the children of previous lessons when they learned that we each must make choices. Ask if they would rather please God or people. Reason with them that to please God, it isn't necessary to have a lot of things. Let them know that it is all right to appreciate and enjoy nice things but that they are not necessary to please God. We should never like what we have more than we like God.

○○○○○

Prayer: Dear Father, Thank you for all the nice things we have that help make us comfortable. Please bless people in other lands so that they have nice things, also. Amen

Parent tip: When you say blessings before meals, include thanks for other things as well as food. Periodically point out to the children how blessed the family is to have the possessions it has. It is helpful to be specific and say, "I'm so glad we have _____." This makes children more aware of the many things they do have and not concentrate on what they do not have. Also this way the children will learn to appreciate what they have and perhaps be more satisfied.

Nobody Likes Me

Scripture verse: "A man that hath friends must shew himself friendly: and there is a friend that sticketh closer than a brother." (Proverbs 18:24, KJV)

Materials needed:

• Slips of paper with "What is one quality you like in a friend?" written on them. Pass these out to selected individuals from the congregation ahead of time and ask them to be prepared to tell one or more qualities they like in a friend.

• Printed copies of the Scripture verse for children to take home

• Materials from previous lessons for "Bumps in the Road of Life"

Procedure: Place a rock on the road labeled "Nobody Likes Me." Using the same procedure as the previous lessons, move the little truck or other chosen object along the road to this bump, and after discussing how to deal with this problem, remove the rock. Let the children know that at some time or another most of us feel that no one likes us. Explain that this is really a feeling of loneliness and probably isn't true. It is good to have friends. We can know that God will always love us, no matter what. Read the following to the children: "But God demonstrates His own love for us in this: While we were still sinners, Christ died for us" (Romans 5:8). We also know that we are never alone because God sees us all the time.

Tell the children that there are some things that everyone likes in others when they choose a friend. If we know what these things are, then we can try to be that way in order to have friends. Ask the adults in the congregation to tell what they like when they choose friends. As the adults read or tell a quality, briefly discuss that quality as time permits.

Introduce the Bible verse: Have the children read the verse together. Explain that "shew" means "show." Usually the things we like in a friend are also the things they like. Ask the people in the congregation to tell the qualities they like in a friend. Then allow the children to add any qualities they can think of. Now, explain that this is the way they should be if they want to have more friends.

Let the children know that a good friend never tries to get you in trouble. Friends should have the best interest of their friends at heart.

OOOOO

Prayer: Dear Jesus, thank you for being a friend to us. Help each of us to be a good friend to others. Amen.

Parent tip: Choose families to associate with who have the same values as you. Try to put your children in positions to make good friends. Don't underestimate the influence of friends on your children.

April

Easter season is a good time to review the basics of acceptance of Christ as personal Savior. The lessons this month deal with belief, knowledge, repentance, and choice.

Can We Believe in Something We Can't See?

Scripture verse: "Blessed are those who have not seen and yet have believed." (John 29:29)

Materials needed:
_____

• Balloons

• Printed copies of Scripture verse for children to take home
_____

Introduce the lesson. Following are suggested questions to stimulate conversation:
_____

• Do you believe there is a God?

• Can you see God?

• Do you believe there is air?

• Can you see air?

• How do we know there is air?
_____

Procedure: Ask a child to blow up a balloon. In case he has a hard time, the teacher may blow up one at the same time.

Ask, "What is going into the balloon? (Air)

Can you see it? (No)

How do you know that air is going into the balloon? (Help the children understand that they see what the air does—it makes the balloon get bigger.)

Let loose of the balloon so the children can see how it moves as the air goes out. Ask, "What makes the balloon move?" (Air leaving the balloon.)

Ask again, "Did you see the air leave the balloon?"

Tell the children that just as we saw the results of the air, we can also see the results of God. Point out that God made flowers, trees, the earth, etc., and we see what he has done. Ask the children to name other things that they know are a result of God. Answers should be things such as the stars, moon, sun, and the love of friends and family.

Introduce the Scripture verse: Pass out copies of today's memory verse. Discuss its meaning in connection with today's activity. Ask the children to repeat the verse a few times together.

Note: You may wish to tell the children that they may have a balloon to take home and that they can pick it up after big church. Ask them to remember as they play with the balloon that God made the air and even though we can't see him, he loves us very much

ooooo

Prayer: "Dear God, help us to believe that you are good and right even though we cannot see you. Thank you for all the wonderful things you have made. Amen."

Parent tip: During the coming week, point out several things that God has given us. When you hug your child, say, "I'm so glad that God gave you to me to love."

God Made the World

Scripture verse: "In the beginning, God created the heavens and the earth." (Genesis 1:1)

Materials needed:

• Printed copies of Scripture verse to hand out

• Talking globe by LeapFrog (You may be able to borrow this from a school or one of the children.)

Procedure: Ask the children if they ever wondered about how the earth came into being and where they came from. Discuss their answers.

Show the globe. Point out that some people talk about a "big bang" theory of how the world was created. Show on the globe how the continents seem to be puzzle pieces that at one time fitted together but are now separated by oceans. Explain that the word "theory" means that something has not been proven.

Read Genesis 1:1–10. Tell the children that the Bible tells us how the world was created and that we have to choose what to believe. We don't know how God did it, but he could have done it with a bang since he did it so fast.

Allow the children to touch the globe with the pen and find out about some of the places God created. Take a little time to let some of the children touch the globe, changing settings occasionally for different information.

Summarize by asking the children if they believe that God is a very great God to have created so very much.

Pat Lamb

Scripture verse: Pass out copies of today's verse and ask the children to repeat it together. Remind them that it is the first verse in the Bible and encourage them to work on memorizing it when they go home.

○○○○○

Prayer: Dear God, thank you for your wonderful creation. Help us to remember that you made everything and to love you more than the things you have made. Amen

Parent tip: During the week, take apart an old clock or watch and show the children the parts on the inside. Ask the children if they think they could have just accidentally come together and work to tell time. Explain that our bodies and the world are much more complicated than a watch or clock and that someone (God) had to put the world and us all together.

3 in 1

Scripture verse: "...and the Holy Spirit descended on him in bodily form like a dove." (Luke 1:22)

Materials needed:

• Three large circles cut from cardboard or any three large circles that can be slit to fit together. On one circle, write the words, "God, the Father," on another circle, "Jesus, the Son," and on the third circle, "Holy Spirit"

• Printed copies of the Scripture verse

Procedure: Ask the children if they know of any time when three can be one. Show the circles, one at a time, and talk about each. Then fit the circles together and explain that now there is only one. Explain that the prefix "tri" means three and that the word trinity means three in unity or three in one. Use the example of a family to further explain. There may be four people in a family, but it is still just one family.

Scripture verse: Read the Scripture verse and ask the children if they know when this happened. Discuss the baptism of Jesus and explain that when we accept Christ as our Savior that the Holy Spirit comes to live inside us. Tell the children that the Bible tells us that the Holy Spirit is a teacher, a comforter, a counselor, and is always inside us to tell us what to do.

Inform the children that when we memorize Scripture, sometimes the Holy Spirit brings Scripture to mind to help us know what we should do when we are in tough situations. Further explain that the Bible says that our bodies are temples. The Holy Spirit dwells inside us as though we are a church, and we should take care of our bodies.

OOOOO

Prayer: Dear Father, help us to always listen for the Holy Spirit to speak to us. Please help us to keep our bodies like a temple for the Spirit to dwell in. Amen.

Parent tip: During the week, talk about how your family members fit together as one unit. Discuss the roles of each family member and compare to the roles of Jesus, God, and the Holy Spirit.

White Dog or Black Dog?

Scripture verse: "...choose for yourselves this day whom you will serve..." (Joshua 24:15)

Materials needed:

• Picture of Jesus

• Picture of Satan (Most children have seen pictures of the devil with a pitchfork, especially around Halloween. Such a picture can be found in several computer programs or perhaps on the Internet. Explain to the children that we really don't know what Satan looks like but someone has made this picture to depict how that person thought he looked. Further explain that the Bible tells us that Satan can make himself look very beautiful in order to trick us.)

• Picture of a white dog

• Picture of a black dog

• Tape or some other means of attaching the pictures to your ears

• A dollar bill

• Printed copies of the Scripture verse

Procedure: Place the picture of the white dog on one ear and the picture of the black dog on your other ear; then tell the following story:

One time there was an Indian chief who was talking to his tribe about choosing to do what is right. He told them that they had a black dog on one shoulder and a white dog on the other. The black dog was always telling the person to do what is wrong. The white dog was always telling the person to do what is right.

"Which way did the person go? Did he act the right way or the wrong way?" asked the people.

The chief answered, "He followed the one that he told 'sic 'em.'"

Explain to the children that "sic 'em" is a term used by many people to tell a dog to go after something. Further explain that this was the chief's way of saying that we choose whom we listen to and follow.

Show the pictures of Jesus and Satan. Take the dogs off and replace them with the pictures of Satan and Jesus. Explain that since there were no cameras in the day when Jesus was on earth that we really don't know what he looked like. Also, tell the children that Satan may look many different ways. Sometimes he looks very attractive.

As the children observe you with the taped pictures on your ears, explain that we always have Jesus on the one hand telling us what to do and the devil on the other hand trying to get us to do what he wants us to do. We have to choose whom we are going to listen to and follow.

Give an example so the children can tell you what the devil would say and what Jesus would say. Place the dollar bill where all can see it. Ask the children to pretend that they are alone with the dollar bill and no one else can see them. Have them tell you what Satan would tell them to do and what Jesus would tell them to do.

Turn your back to the dollar bill and close your eyes. Ask the children if they are being tempted to take the money since they know you are not looking. Ask what Jesus wants them to do and what Satan wants them to do. Turn back around.

Tell the children that the phrase "the devil made me do it" is not true. God gives us each a right to choose and holds us responsible for our choices. Good choices have good results; bad choices have bad results. God sees us all the time and does not excuse us because of age. Remind them of the Bible verse: "Even a child is known by his doing" (Prov. 20:11).

Present the plan of salvation. Explain that it is easy to choose Jesus. We must believe that Jesus is the Son of God and came to earth and died on the cross for us, be sorry for our sins, and ask God to save us. The Holy Spirit will come into our hearts if we ask him to do so but not unless we really mean it. Tell the children to bow their heads in prayer and if they really want to be saved to pray the following prayer with you.

Note: Arrangements may need to be made for the children to talk further with the pastor or counselor.

OOOOO

Prayer: "Dear God, I believe that you sent your Son, Jesus, to die on the cross for me. I am really sorry for my sins. Please forgive me and send the Holy Spirit to live in me. I want to live for you and not serve the devil. Please help me to do that."

Scripture verse: Pass out copies of today's memory verse. Simply read it as it is being passed out. To do more might disrupt the current feelings that the children probably are experiencing.

Parent tip: Pray with the children during the week and be prepared to answer questions they may have about salvation. You may want to schedule an appointment with the pastor for further counseling or scheduling of baptism.

May

Our minds naturally turn to mothers during this month, so it is a good time to emphasize a mother's love and the family unit. At the end of the month, Memorial Day is celebrated, and we don't want to neglect to recognize our indebtedness to those who fought for our freedom. Memorial Day is also a good time to think about our heritage. Children need to understand that things don't just happen. People in the past have worked hard for us to have what we have.

Love Is Forever

Scripture verse: "…let us love one another, for love comes from God." (1 John 4:7)

Materials needed:

• Children's book *Love You Forever* by Robert Munsch

• Printed copies of the Scripture verse

Procedure: Discuss with the children that love is something we do, not just something we feel. Sometimes people do things we don't like but that doesn't mean that we stop loving them. Mothers and fathers should love their children always no matter what they do and children should always love their parents as well.

Introduce and read the book, Love You Forever by Robert Munsch. (This is a very powerful book. When I used it, the congregation got very quiet and seemed to be getting as much from it as the children. I did make up a tune for the repetitive part and sang that part whenever I came to it. You may find that helpful. If you don't feel comfortable singing that part, you might ask another person to do it for you. It should be done very softly, similar to a lullaby.)

Tell the children that God will always love us and that when we hurt, it is as though he puts his arms around us to comfort us.

Introduce the Scripture verse: Give each child a copy of the Scripture verse and say it together several times.

OOOOO

Prayer: Dear Father, thank you for always loving us. Help us to love others just as you love us. Amen.

Parent tip: Talk to your children to assure them that you will always love them.

However, let them know that some things they might do would hurt you very much. When we love people, we don't want to hurt them. We should try to please God because we love him. It is all right to let the children know that you hope they will love you enough that they would not want to hurt you.

Love Is Something You Do!

(Mother's Day Lesson)

Scripture verse: "Love thy father and thy mother." (Exodus 20:12, KJV)

Materials needed:

• Banner: "Love is something you do." (Note: Print Shop Deluxe computer program has a stretch dog that works nicely for this banner.)

• Flip chart

• Sticker Scripture verses to hand out to the children with today's verse for the children to memorize

Procedure: Ask the children to tell what special day this is and have a short discussion of how they are celebrating this day. Since grandparents, instead of mothers, are raising many children at this time in our country, mention that some people act as mothers when the real mother is not able to do so. Ask the children if they love their mothers or grandmothers, and if so, how they show it.

Display the banner.

Tell the children that it is easy to say that we love someone but that real love requires showing love by our actions. Using the flip chart, ask the children to name all the ways they can think of that mothers and grandmothers show love to their children. An older child may write the answers or the child who names something may come up and write if they want. Do not wait for the child to write, but rather discuss while the writing is taking place in order to save time.

After discussing how mothers show love, ask the children to name the ways that a child can show love to the mother or grandmother. Using the same procedure, list those ways and discuss.

Review the items listed.

Tell the children again that love is something we do, not just something we feel or say.

Scripture verse: Hand out the copies of the Scripture verse and have the children repeat the verse together.

○○○○○

Prayer: Dear Jesus, help us to show our love to mothers, grandmothers, or others who are caring for us. Amen.

Parent tip: Dad, you need to work with your children to help them respect and appreciate their mother. During the week, point out several things that Mom does to show her love and encourage the children to tell her thanks and to show respect for her. You may also need to help them make or choose gifts for their mother.

On Your Honor

Scripture verse: "Honor your father and your mother…" (Exodus 20:12)

Materials needed:

• A basket or box from which children can draw a slip of paper

• Slips of paper with descriptions of family situations:

> • Mother has just done the laundry and taken the folded clean clothes to her son's room for him to put away. When she does the laundry the next time, she discovers that some of the clean clothes have been placed in the dirty clothesbasket.

> • Dad has just prepared the evening meal and calls his daughter to the table. He has called her three times, and she still hasn't come.

> • James was in the house when his mother drove up from grocery shopping. He knew she would need help, so he went to the car and helped carry the groceries in.

> • Susan helps clear the table after meals without being asked. Each family member carries his or her own dishes to the kitchen after eating.

> • Last time Jerry's mom asked him to do something, he ignored her. When she repeated the request, he said, "Why do I have to do that? I'm busy!"

• Whenever Janie and her mom go shopping, Janie continually talks about what the other girls have and asks her mom for many new clothes. Her mother seldom buys anything for herself.

• Judy likes to talk. When her mom and dad talk, she often interrupts.

• Bobby comes home from school and immediately does his homework. He is on a schedule and does not argue about it.

• When Sherry visits a friend's home, she calls her mom as soon as she gets there to let her know she got there okay.

• Frank is very careful to take care of his belongings. He keeps them where they belong and uses them properly.

• Printed copies of the Scripture verse

Procedure: Tell the children that today we will talk about honoring parents. To honor our parents means to show respect. We need to remember that they have more experience than we have and listen to what they have to say. We often say we love our parents, but our actions show how we really feel.

Show the box with the slips of paper. Ask a child to draw out a slip and read it. (You will need to use your judgment as to whether the child reads or you read.) Have the children decide if the person mentioned is showing honor to parents.

Continue having children draw out the slips of paper

and discussing them as time permits.

Introduce the Bible verse. Tell the children that today's Bible verse is one of the Ten Commandments. It is very important to remember it. Ask them to repeat it several times with you.

○○○○○

Prayer: Dear Father, please forgive us for the times we have not shown honor to our parents or those who have authority over us. Thank you for people who care for us, especially parents. Please remind us to do better in honoring our parents or those who care for us in the future. Amen.

Parent tip: Occasionally drop hints to your children to help them realize times they can be helpful without being told outright to do something. It is always best to have the child make the right decision. You might say something like, "My, these groceries are heavy!" or "I don't know if I'll be able to do _____." If the hints don't work, then go ahead and ask children to help.

I'm Important to My Family

Scripture verse: "…But as for me and my household, we will serve the Lord." (Joshua 24:15)

Materials needed:

- Flannel board with cutout of house, father, mother, sister, and brother

- Printed copies of the Scripture verse

- Four pieces of string or yarn approximately eighteen inches long for each child

Procedure: Have the flannel board and cutouts in place to begin. Ask the children to describe what they think makes a good family that is pleasing to God. Ask what happens when one person in the family decides to go his/her own way and not be with the family. (On the flannel board, place one child away from the group with back turned.)

Ask, "Does the action of this one person affect only him or does it affect the entire family?"

Explain that God created the family and he wants us to all work together as a team to serve him. Ask what happens on a basketball team if one person just keeps the ball to himself and doesn't cooperate with the other players. Is more accomplished by the one or if they all play together?

Ask the children if they have chores to do at home. What happens if they don't do their chores? Show that it affects the whole family. For instance, if the chore is to empty trash and it isn't done, the house may get smelly and seem messy and everyone has to put up with it.

Ask the children to take a piece of string and see if they can break it. Then ask them to put two pieces of string together and see if they can break it. Then ask the children to put three pieces of string together and see if they can break it. If someone can still break the three pieces, ask that person to put four pieces of string together and try to break it.

Ask the children which was easier to break, the one piece or more than one piece. Relate this to the family to show that when a family sticks together, it is hard to break it apart.

Explain to the children that God does not want sisters and brothers to fuss and argue. We need to stick together as families and help each other. There is enough hardship outside the family. The family should be a safe place. Family members are tied together with blood. There is a special bond. Brothers and sisters should honor their parents and each other.

(Place the family member back with the family.) Say, "When the family is all together, it is much nicer. We each have a part to play in making our family a family that pleases God."

Scripture verse: Hand out copies of the memory verse and ask the children to repeat it together several times. Suggest that they take it home and put it someplace where they can see it often and work on memorizing it during the week.

OOOOO

Prayer: Dear Father, please forgive us for the times we have argued with our brothers and sisters. Please forgive us for the times we have disobeyed and help me to be a good family member. Amen.

Parent tip: Sometimes children argue with each other because they feel the other is being favored such as in the story of Joseph and his coat of many colors. Be sure the children understand that you love each one as much as the other.

Remembering Those Who Helped Us

(Suitable for Memorial Day)

Scripture verse: "…Choose for yourselves this day whom you will serve." (Joshua 24:15)

Materials needed:

• A military item or items (A military uniform is excellent.)

• Pictures of persons in military uniform or an actual individual dressed in uniform

• Ribbon to use as a dividing line for good and bad

• Two signs: one that says "good" and one that says "evil"

• Copies of the Scripture verse for children to take home

Procedure: Ask the children if they know what holiday we are celebrating and the reason for celebrating this holiday. Discuss the meaning of the holiday.

Tell the children that ever since God created people he has expected persons to choose between good and evil. Explain that sometimes people choose to follow the devil and not to follow God. Explain that some people do evil things and try to take away the freedom of others. Further explain that all through the ages there have been wars and that sometimes our country has had to go to war to protect its freedom.

Show the military items. If a uniform is available, allow the children to try on the jacket if they so desire. Some children may want to tell about people they know who are in the military. List the things that military people do such as give up comfort, obey orders, possibly give up life itself, etc. Ask the children if they appreciate the things that have been done so that we can enjoy freedom. Encourage them to name some things that they are free to do such as go to church, go to school, say what they feel like saying, etc.

Tell the children that many other people have helped us in the past as well as military people. Talk about political leaders, forefathers, and parents. Mention that we each have a responsibility to do what we can to be good.

Place the ribbon vertically to the children and place a sign that says good and another that says evil on each side of the ribbon. Ask the children to stand on the side they choose.

Introduce the Bible verse and ask the children to repeat it a few times.

(If this lesson is being used in "big church," it would be nice to ask all veterans in the congregation from each branch of the military service [one branch at a time] to stand and be recognized. If it is being used at home or elsewhere, make arrangements for the children to meet a real veteran.)

Scripture verse: Since this verse was used earlier, it should be easier for the children to say.

OOOOO

Prayer: Dear Father, thank you for those who have fought for our freedom. Please help us to think carefully and choose wisely. Amen.

Parent Tip: Take your children to a museum that displays military equipment and discuss it with them.

June

June is a time to think of dad and his role in the family. How distressing it is to learn that one third of the wives in this country are verbally abused. It follows that if fathers are abusing their wives, they are capable of abusing their children also. It is difficult to teach children to respect, obey, and love abusive fathers, but we must point out the ideal way as the Scripture tells us.

Earthly fathers should ideally be a reflection of the heavenly Father. Can we get this across to children and eavesdropping dads?

A Loving Father

Scripture verse: "For God so loved the world that he gave his only begotten son that whosoever believeth in him should not perish but have everlasting life." (John 3:16, KJV)

Objective: To help children realize the great love that our heavenly Father demonstrated when he gave his son for us.

Materials needed:

• A striker

• A candle

• Aluminum foil

• Three or four dead bugs

• Printed copies of the Scripture verse

The following questions may help to open the discussion:

• How many fathers do you have? (Children may say they have one or may include stepfathers. Most children will not readily realize that they have both a heavenly Father and an earthly father.)

• Do you love your father?

• Should your father love you?

• What is love? Does it mean that you like someone who likes you?

• Can you love someone who doesn't like you?

Procedure: Show the striker and if necessary show a candle and demonstrate how it is used to light a candle. Be sure to advise children to never play with it.

Ask if they have one at home and how they use it. Ask if they have ever been burned by fire. Use the striker to burn the dead bugs over the aluminum foil. Tell the children that the bugs have perished.

Introduce the Bible verse and go over the verse with the children and explain how God loved us so much, even though we didn't even know him, that he gave his only son so we would not perish. Help the children understand that it took a lot of love to give a son for someone who was a sinner. Explain that it is necessary for us to believe that Jesus died on the cross to be saved so we will not perish.

Point out that earthly fathers are supposed to love their children as our heavenly Father loves us. Help the children understand that earthly fathers are not perfect and sometimes make mistakes, but we can love them anyway.

Introduce the Scripture verse: Ask the children to repeat the Scripture verse several times. Take each part and explain it. Be sure to give the meanings of any words they do not understand.

OOOOO

Prayer: Ask the children to repeat the words after you in the following prayer:

Dear God,

Thank you for sending your son to die for me.
I believe that Jesus died on the cross.
Please forgive me for my sins and come into
my heart.
Amen.

Parent tip: Dads, this week take your children on your lap and tell them that you love them. Apologize for anything that you have done wrong to them.

It Isn't Nice to Heckle

Scripture verse: "It is more blessed to give than to receive."
(Acts 20:35)

Materials needed:

• Printed Scripture verses to hand out to children

Procedure:
Tell the following story:

"Mary's Birthday Wish"

In Albuquerque, New Mexico, there lived a little girl
named Mary. Mary liked birthdays more than anything in the world. She enjoyed helping her mother
bake cakes and decorate them with icing of different
colors. Sometimes they would bake cakes that looked
like trains, dolls, or even rabbits. Mary enjoyed all
birthdays very much, but the one she especially liked
was her own.

Mary's birthday was in June when school was out
for the summer. Her family was usually vacationing on
June 28th, the day of her birthday. Mary spent birthdays in places like Missouri, Colorado, and one very
special one in Mexico. This year, however, Mary's parents had decided to stay home during June, and they
would not be traveling on her birthday. Mary looked
forward to being home for her birthday because this
year her mom would bake a cake for her. Mary began
making plans a month early. She calculated daily how

many shopping days her family had left for buying presents.

Mary loved her dad very much and always enjoyed joking with him. As her birthday grew closer, she became curious about what kind of presents she would be getting. She really wanted a pretty blue bike, one that she had seen at the store. Mary's family was very good at keeping secrets, and nobody would tell her anything about what she was going to get. When she asked her dad about her present, he would always say, "You are getting a bundle of switches." Back in her dad's time, when he got in trouble, he sometimes got spanked with small tree branches that fell from the tree. They called them switches. Mary knew her dad was kidding and laughed when he would give that answer.

Mary's birthday drew nearer and nearer. One Saturday morning, on grocery shopping day, Mary got up especially early because this was the last grocery day before her birthday. Mary went to the store with her mom and picked out which flavor birthday cake she wanted. Her mom promised to make a very special cake for her.

The next four days went by slowly. Finally, Wednesday, June 28, came, and Mary woke early. She was very excited and felt a year older. Mary's mother had planned for Mary and her three brothers to go swimming all day while she got things ready for her birthday dinner that night.

When Mary and her brothers came back from the pool, they had to wait about an hour for their dad to come home from work. Finally, her father pulled into the driveway in his pickup truck. Mary squealed with joy and squinted her eyes to see if something was in the back of his truck for her, but there was nothing there.

All through supper, Mary was very excited and held in suspense about her presents. She gulped down her food hastily and waited for the rest of her family to finish.

After what seemed to be hours, everyone finished eating. It was time to open presents. One by one, each of her brothers gave her something they had carefully chosen at the store. At last there was only one present left to open...the one from her parents.

Everyone told her, "Hold out your hands and close your eyes and you will get a big surprise." Mary heard someone exit the room, and she knew it must be something big. She held her hands way out and finally felt something press down on her arms. Mary opened her eyes and there it was, a great big, huge, bundle of switches wrapped with a blue ribbon. Mary looked to the ground feeling sad and ashamed that she had heckled her dad so much about her present. She thought he had decided not to get her anything.

As she looked down at the kitchen floor, tears began to fill her eyes. She heard her oldest brother, Ken, leave the room, and after a minute she worked up the nerve to look her dad in the face. He was smiling at her. She heard the kitchen door open and there was her older brother.

Ken was pushing a bike, a brand new bike, the very same blue bike she wanted. Mary was both excited and relieved in the same instant. She gave her mom and dad huge hugs and kisses and told them thank you.

She took her bike outside and rode around. Then, she remembered she had forgotten something.

Mary parked her bike and ran inside, and there was her mother holding the most beautiful birthday cake Mary had ever seen. It looked like a doll. Her father took out some matches and lit the candles, and her family all sang "Happy Birthday" to her.

Mary was very happy when she went to bed that night. Before going to sleep, she prayed to thank God for her wonderful family, her birthday, and especially for her brand new bike. Mary never heckled anyone about what she was going to get for her birthday again.

Ask the children what Mary learned from her experience. Tell them that it is not nice to always be asking for something as some children do when they go shopping with parents.

Introduce the Scripture verse: Tell the children that Jesus wants us to think of others more than ourselves, and when we heckle others, it is a sign that we are only thinking of ourselves.

○○○○○

Prayer: Dear Father, even though it is hard for us to do, please help us to think of others more than ourselves. Amen.

Parent tip: Sometimes we need to be creative in our teaching methods. Telling is not teaching. A child must understand the wrong and right of a situation in order to truly learn.

Truth Is Smarter

Scripture verse: "Keep your tongue from evil and your lips from speaking lies." (Psalm 34:13)

Materials needed:

• A jar or pitcher of water colored with orange food coloring

• Paper cups

• Paper towel to collect spills

• Printed memory verses to hand out

Procedure: Tell the following story:

One time there was a little girl whose father owned a grocery store. This store had two big display windows in front, and in one window her father placed some gallons of pretty orange drink. They were stacked prettily so that when people walked by the store, they would see them and hopefully come in to buy some of the pretty orange drink.

The little girl really wanted some of the orange drink. She asked her daddy if she could have some, but he told her that it was for customers to buy and that if the family drank it, there would not be any left to sell.

The little girl thought about this, and the more she thought, the more she knew that the orange drink would really taste good and the more she wanted to try some.

The little girl waited until no one was around and then quietly slipped up to the window, took one of the gallons of drink, opened it, and drank some. Then she put the lid back on and put it back in the window. She was silly to think that no one would notice some of the drink gone!

People walked by the window and looked at the pretty orange drink. The jar on top was not full.

Soon her daddy came, and he, too, noticed that the top jar was not full. He called all of the children together and asked them who had drunk some of the drink. No one confessed. Even the little girl, fearing that she was in trouble, lied to her father and told him that she had not done it.

Finally, the little girl began to feel guilty and confessed that she had really wanted some of the drink and that she had taken it. Of course, the little girl got a hard spanking for doing such a naughty thing.

Tell the children you brought something to drink. Show the pretty jar of colored water. Pour each of them a small amount in a paper cup and allow them to taste it.

When they find that the taste was not as expected, explain that many times in life things that we thought would be great do not turn out as expected. Inform them that they just drank colored water.

Instruct the children that it is best not to give in to temptation, but when it does happen, it is best to tell the truth rather than do two things wrong.

Introduce the Bible verse: Read today's verse several times together.

OOOOO

Prayer: Dear heavenly Father, thank you for our daddies

who teach us right from wrong. Please help us to be strong and to resist temptation. Help us to always tell the truth. Amen.

Parent tip: It would be good for dads to think of a story from their own lives to tell their children about a time when a lie caused more trouble. Be sure that you always set a good example of honesty in all dealings with family and business.

I Love My Daddy

Scripture verse: "Children, obey your parents in the Lord, for this is right." (Ephesians 6:1)

Materials needed:

• 9x11 letters spelling out F-A-T-H-E-R

• Notes on the back of the letters saying the following:

  • F…Forgiving

  • A…Always understanding

  • T…There when I need him

  • H…Helpful

  • E…Energetic enough to play with me

  • R…Respects me

• Printed copies of the Scripture verse

Procedure: Ask the following questions:

• How would you describe a really good dad?

• What things have you seen dads do that you liked?

• Do you like it when you see dads playing with kids?

• Do you like it when you see dads listening to their children?

• Do you like it when you see dads telling stories to their children?

• Do you like it when dads listen to their children before scolding them?

• Do you like it when dads help with homework?

• Do you like it when dads talk to kids like grownups?

After discussing the above questions, tell the children that the things can be summed up with words indicated on the 9x11 letters. Read each letter and the note on the back, explaining the meanings as you go. Have individual children hold up the letters facing the congregation if this is done in "big church," or their classmates if the lesson is used in Sunday school, to spell out F-A-T-H-E-R. If this lesson is done at home, simply have the children make a poster or greeting card to show to their father.

Introduce the Scripture verse: Discuss the verse and hand out copies for the children to take home and memorize.

ooooo

Prayer: Dear heavenly Father, thank you for our fathers you have given us here on earth. Help me to show respect for my father and to obey him. Amen.

Parent tip: The Bible says for children to obey parents in the right. Sometimes parents make it difficult for children to obey. Be sure what you are asking the child to do is in the right. Moms, plan with the children ways to make Father's Day special for dad.

July

After lessons about the home and family, we begin a series of lessons to help develop self-discipline. We must first, however, have a lesson on patriotism to help children appreciate the true meaning of Independence Day celebration. The lessons on self-discipline will carry over into August. By learning to control one part of the body at a time, children can eventually learn to control the entire body. These lessons can also develop an appreciation of God's creation of the human body and stimulate motivation for good health habits in caring for God's temple, the human body.

Respect

(Appropriate for Independence Day)

Scripture verse: "Give to Caesar what is Caesar's, and to God what is God's." (Matthew 22:21)

Materials needed:

• Printed Scripture verses for children to take home

• Small purchased U.S. flags to give to children

• Chart tablet or other writing surface

Procedure: Write the word "respect" on the chart tablet and ask the children to discuss the meaning of the word. An older child may write key words of the definitions.

Then, have the children name things for which we should show respect. Such words as parent, teachers, ministers, opinions and belongings of others, and the U.S. flag will hopefully be given.

Show the flag and have the children count the stripes and stars. Tell them that the thirteen stripes represent the thirteen colonies and the fifty stars represent the fifty states. The children will probably not know what a colony was and you will need to tell them. After discussing the flag, give each child a flag as a reminder to honor our country and flag.

If time permits, a person may be invited to tell how to properly care for a flag. The local VFW chapter would probably be glad to have someone come and do that.

Briefly inform the children that our country is free because of the sacrifices many people have made. Not all people in the world enjoy the same freedom as we do and some people do not believe in Jesus. People who haven't learned to think of others often cause trouble. Sometimes wars are necessary to protect us from people who would destroy our freedom. When our country first started, the Declaration of Independence was written and a war was fought so we could be free. The Fourth of July is the day set aside to celebrate our freedom.

Ask the veterans in the congregation to stand for the children to see the people near them who have served in the military to protect our freedom. If time permits, recognize those veterans from each branch of the service.

Introduce the Scripture verse: Jesus told us to respect our leaders. Explain the background story of the verse. Ask the children to repeat the verse several times.

ooooo

Prayer: Dear Father, thank you for our leaders. Please give them wisdom to lead as you would have them to do. Help us to show respect for them and to obey the laws as we should. Amen.

Parent tip: Be careful with conversation around home when speaking about the leaders of our country. We should talk about leaders with respect even when we disagree with them. It is difficult for children to respect their country if they hear their parents speaking badly about it.

Hearing Ears

Scripture verse: "He who has ears, let him hear." (Matthew 11:15)

Materials needed:

• Paper cup telephone made by using a string between two paper or foam cups

• A few paper bags with various substances in each one. In each bag put a different material such as rice, small stones, small bells, beans, cotton balls, etc.

• Printed copies of the Scripture verse

Questions appropriate for introducing the lesson:

• Have you ever thought what it would be like to not be able to hear?

• Do you know anyone who is deaf?

• Do you know any sign language?

• Who made our ears and gave us the ability to hear?

• Is it possible to use our ears in a bad way? How? (We can listen to gossip, wrong music, bad language, etc.)

Procedure: Show the paper cup telephone. Let the children try it out. Tell them that at one time there were no real telephones. People could only write letters and send them by messenger. Now we can hear people from many miles away by using the telephone.

Ask the children if they are good listeners. Using the paper bags with various items, shake them, one at a time, and ask the children to guess what is inside.

Explain that although we have the ability to hear, we don't always hear because we do not listen. Explain that it is important to listen to the preacher in church and not listen to the person sitting beside you. Tell them that Jesus told some people to use their ears to hear.

Sing "Be Careful, Little Ears." After singing it once, ask the children to sing it with you. If you do not know the tune, simply read the following words:

> Be careful, little ears, what you hear,
> Be careful, little ears, what you hear.
> There's a Father up above
> Looking down on you with love,
> So be careful, little ears, what you hear.

Introduce the Scripture verse: Discuss the verse and have the children say it with you several times.

OOOOO

Prayer: Dear Father, help us to learn to listen carefully when others speak. Help us to especially pay attention to our parents, pastor, and teachers. Amen.

Parent tip: Play the game "gossip" at home with your children. Most people are familiar with this game. One person whispers something in the ear of the person sitting next to him or her, and each person passes it on by whispering. The last person then tells what he or she thought was said at the beginning. This illustrates the importance of listening carefully and getting information straight.

My Feet Are Neat

Scripture verse: "Your Word is a lamp to my feet and a light for my path." (Psalm 119:105)

Materials needed:

• A few pairs of shoes of various sizes and colors

• Optional: A chart showing the skeletal structure of the foot. This can probably be obtained from a doctor's office or the science teacher at school. Many skeletal pictures are also available on the Internet.

• Printed copies of the Scripture verse

Questions appropriate for introducing the lesson:

Younger Children:

• How many feet do you have?

• Who made your feet?

• Why do you think God gave us feet?

• Do your feet always obey?

• Do your feet always go to good places?

• When your mommy or daddy tells you not to go someplace and you go anyway, are your feet going to the right place?

• Your feet may not always do what your parents tell you to do, but do they always do what you tell them to do?

• Do you think we should be careful what we tell our feet to do?

Older Children:

• What do you know about feet? (Answers may include "they get tired," "they hurt when shoes are too small," or "some feet are big," etc.)

• Do your feet decide where they will go or do you have to tell them?

• Where can feet take you?

• What determines where feet take you?

Procedure: Show the various shoes and talk about the different styles of shoes that are used for different purposes. Bring out how remarkable it is that God made each foot with five toes, lots of bones, tendons, etc. (If the chart of the foot's skeletal structure is available, show it here.) Emphasize that God knew just what he was doing when he designed feet. Continue to get the point across that we, not the shoes, determine where the feet go. Ask the children to name some good places that feet can go and some places that feet should not go.

Teach the song "Be Careful, Little Feet." (If you do not know the song, simply read the words.)

> Be careful, little feet, where you go.
> Be careful, little feet, where you go.
> There's a Father up above
> Looking down on you with love,
> So be careful, little feet, where you go.

Tell the children that the Bible tells us where our feet should and should not go.

Introduce the Bible verse: Explain the verse and repeat it together several times.

OOOOO

Prayer: Dear Father, thank you for giving us brains so that we can control our bodies. Help me to tell my feet to go to the right places. Amen.

Parent tip: During the week, as you are driving here and there, point out places that are good and not good for us to go. Mention that it is good to go to church, but it is not good to go to bars, etc. Explain to the children why it is not good to go some places while it is good to go other places.

Using Our Tongues to Praise

Scripture verse: "With the tongue we praise our Lord and Father..." (James 3:9)

Materials needed:

• Pictures of lips or happy smiling faces with different expressions such as an upturned mouth or a mouth turned down with a frown

• A tube of lipstick and a piece of paper to draw a picture of a tongue

• A dollar bill

• Printed copies of the Scripture verse

Questions to be used to introduce the lesson:

• Why did God give us a mouth?

• What do we use our mouths for?

• What is inside our mouths?

• Has anyone ever said anything to you that made you feel badly?

• Has anyone ever said anything to you to make you feel really great?

• How do you like for people to talk to you?

• Do you like them to say kind things to you?

• Have you ever said anything unkind to someone else?

• Do you remember a time when you said something good to someone and they looked happy?

Procedure: After asking the above questions, show the
pictures of the different faces and ask the children to
identify the feelings expressed by the faces.

Using the lipstick, draw a simple picture of a tongue
to emphasize the fact that it is the tongue that makes it
possible for us to talk. Tell the children that God expects
us to use the tongue wisely and that the Bible tells us to
be kind to others.

Ask the children to tell some nice things that could
be said about others. Point out that we should never say
things to make others feel badly such as criticizing what
is being worn or how someone looks.

Introduce the Bible verse: Tell the children that the
very best thing we can do with our tongues is to praise
Jesus and God. Ask the children to share good things that
they can say about Jesus and God. As they name things,
attempt to remember them to use in the closing prayer.
They should say such things as, "Jesus loves us," "God
loves us," "God made pretty things for us to enjoy," "God
takes care of us," "Jesus died for us," etc.

OOOOO

Prayer: Dear Father, thank you for loving and caring for
us. Thank you for all of the pretty things you have made.
Most of all, thank you for loving us so much that you sent
your Son to die for us. Amen.

Parent tip: Be very careful how you speak in front of
children. They learn by example.

Caring Hands

Scripture verse: "Whatever your hand finds to do, do it with all your might." (Ecclesiastes 9:10)

Materials needed:

• Several different gloves for the children to try on (Work gloves, dress gloves, mittens, and other gloves will help the children see different uses of the hands.)

• Copies of today's Bible verse for children to take home

Questions to use to introduce the topic:

Younger children:

• How many hands do you have?

• How many fingers do you have on each hand?

• Do you have gloves or mittens for your hands?

• What are some of the things we do with our hands?

Older children:

• What are some good things we can do with our hands?

• What are some things we should not do with our hands? (Children may name such things as stealing, making messes in the house, damaging property of others, etc.)

Procedure: After discussing the above questions, tell the children that since they are young, they have more energy than older people and that they can be a big help by picking up things, putting away things, or running to get things.

Place a dollar bill on the floor in front of the children and ask them what they should do about it. Help them to understand that they should never take anything that does not belong to them and that they should not touch things that are not theirs no matter how much they are tempted to do so.

Introduce Bible verse: Tell the children that we should keep our hands busy doing good things. Read the verse and explain it. Ask the children to repeat it together. Ask how many will try to use their hands to help others.

OOOOO

Prayer: Dear Father, please help us to have helping hands and to use our hands wisely. Amen

Parent tip: Be sure to praise children when they use their hands to pick up and put away things around the house. If time permits, plan and make a craft project to give to someone. Talk to the children about using our hands to serve others.

August

In August, we can continue to teach self-discipline by doing lessons about individual body parts. Since schools usually start toward the end of August or the beginning of September, it is good to include some lessons to help get the children thinking about learning. In keeping with this thought, the last lesson of the month is "Do Your Best to Learn."

Growing Strong Bodies

Scripture verse: "But Daniel resolved not to defile himself with the royal food and wine…" (Daniel 1:8)

Materials needed:

• A bag of chips, a package of cookies, and a can of Coke, a small tray of vegetables such as carrot and celery sticks

• A baggie with ten teaspoons of sugar to show the amount of sugar in a standard-size Coke (Twenty-three teaspoons of sugar for a large Mountain Dew, etc. Four grams of sugar equals one teaspoon if you want to figure amounts for other items.)

• Printed copies of the Scripture verse for the children to take home

Procedure: Tell the story of Daniel as given in the first chapter of Daniel. Then ask the following questions:

• Was Daniel required to eat vegetables or did he choose to eat them?

• What kind of food do you think the king wanted Daniel to eat?

• Why do you think that Daniel chose vegetables?

• Why are vegetables better for us than rich food?

(Explain that rich food means foods that have a lot of fat and sugar like cake and cookies.)

Procedure: Discuss the questions. Point out that fat and sugar are not always good for us.

Show the items brought. Read part of the labels to the children. Explain that four grams of sugar equals one teaspoon of sugar. Show the baggie containing the sugar to show how much sugar is in a Coke. Give them further information that 3500 calories equals one pound of fat. If we take in 3500 calories that we don't use, we gain one pound of fat. Read the calories on the labels. Tell them that vegetables don't have many calories.

If we do much physical activity, we need more calories than if we are not very active. Explain that Daniel knew that it is important to be in good physical condition in order to better serve God. He knew that we should eat what we need and not necessarily what we want.

Ask the children to choose from the items on display the ones that are good for them and those that are not.

Introduce the verse: Ask the children to repeat the verse several times with you.

OOOOO

Prayer: Dear Father, thank you for all of the wonderful foods you have made for us. Please help us to be wise in choosing the right foods for what our bodies need and not just think of what we want. Please give us strong, healthy bodies so that we might better serve you. Amen.

Parent tip: Make a special effort to serve healthy foods to your child. Try to see that there are plenty of vegetables available and praise the children when they make good food choices. When they ask for extra food, say, "Do you think you really need that?" Remove things from your home that are not good for your children. As they eat, teach them the value of foods as you are able. For example, carrots and all yellow foods have vitamin A and are good for the eyes.

A Good Heart

Scripture verse: "Keep thy heart with all diligence; for out of it are the issues of life." (Proverbs 4:23, KJV)

Materials needed:

• Printed Scripture verses for children to take home

• A picture of the anatomy of the human heart (Can be obtained on the Internet by typing in "heart anatomy.")

Procedure: Ask the children to put their hands on their chest to feel their heart beating. Show them how to take their pulse in the wrist.

Show the picture of the human heart. Point out some of the parts and briefly explain how the heart pumps the blood through the body. Have them look at the veins in their arms and tell them that the heart pumps the blood through those blood vessels to all parts of the body. There are miles of blood vessels for the heart to service. When we get fat, the heart has to work harder to get the blood through the blood vessels. God wants us to take care of our hearts by eating right and staying physically active. We should never use bad drugs because they can affect the heart.

The word "heart" has another meaning. It means the center of something. The heart is mentioned many times in the Bible, as in today's verse, to mean the center of our soul. We need to have a pure heart. We can't see this heart with our eyes, but God talks about it very much. It means our attitude of love, our desire to do what is right to please God, and our thoughts.

We can make our hearts pleasing to God by believing that he sent his Son to die on the cross for us, being sorry for our sins, and asking God to send the Holy Spirit to live inside us. This will not happen unless we really want it to. God can read our minds. He looks at our hearts and knows everything about us, so we can't trick him.

Ask the children if they would like to make their hearts pleasing to God. Tell them that if they really mean it, to pray the following prayer with you.

> Dear God, I believe that you sent your only Son, Jesus, to die on the cross for me. I am really sorry for my sins. Please come into my heart. Amen.

Introduce the Scripture verse: Tell the children that even though God forgives our sins, we continue to be tempted as long as we live. It is necessary for us to continually guard our thoughts and feelings to keep our hearts pure. To be diligent means that we don't forget to do what we should do. We keep at it. When we make mistakes, we need to again go to God to ask for forgiveness. If our hearts are pure, we make good decisions.

If our hearts are not pure, we make bad decisions. The "issues of life" means things that come up that we have to deal with. It is really important that we keep our hearts right before God.

ⵔⵔⵔⵔⵔ

Prayer again: Dear Father, thank you for sending the Holy Spirit to live in the hearts of those who want him to do so. Please help us keep our hearts pure by learning Scripture and praying. Amen.

Parent tip: Have a daily Bible study at home and encourage the children to confess daily sins in their bedtime prayers.

Brain Power

Scripture verse: "The heart of the righteous studieth to answer: but the mouth of the wicked poureth out evil things." (Proverbs 15:28, KJV)

Materials needed:

• A printed copy of today's Scripture verse for each child

• A school textbook

• A puzzle

• A board game such as Monopoly or Balderdash

• Ask a child in advance to bring a LeapFrog product to the group.

Procedure: Remind the children that it is almost time for school to start. Ask if they feel they are ready to go back to school.

Give information about school when Jesus was a little boy to let them know that Jesus also had to attend school to learn the Scriptures.

Give a brief listing of some of the things studied this month and the previous month about using the different parts of our bodies to please Jesus. Remind them that God made our brains and he wants us to use them wisely also.

Ask, "How can we make our brains think well?"

Explain that brains need to be exercised just like the remainder of the body. There are things we can do to help us think well. Show the items listed above. Help the children understand that reading, playing games, and studying help our minds to develop. Encourage the children to start reading now before school starts to help them remember some of the things they may have forgotten during the summer.

Introduce the Scripture verse: Explain that when people talked during the time that the King James Bible was translated, they often put an "eth" on the end of the word. Ask the children to put their finger over the "eth" on the word "poureth" in the printed verse and tell you what the word is that they see.

Explain the meaning of the verse and tell the children God expects us to think and study so that what we say is wise and not foolish. Some people just talk a lot and really don't make sense. God doesn't want us to be like that.

OOOOO

Prayer: Dear heavenly Father, please help us think clearly and use our brains to study and learn. Thank you for giving us the ability to think and reason. Amen.

Parent tip: Put together puzzles and play board games with your children. Choose toys that teach. Do a lot of counting with your child and help the child figure out the cost of various items.

Do Your Best to Learn

Scripture verse: "Study to show thyself approved unto God..." (2 Timothy 2:15, KJV)

Materials needed:

- Printed Scripture verses

- Banner with Scripture verse

- Scissors

Procedure: Tell the children that attending school is a real opportunity that we should appreciate and that many children in the world are not able to attend school. Explain that God wants us to learn so that we can be good witnesses for him.

Show the banner containing the Scripture verse. Ask the children to read the banner. Explain the meaning of the word "approved." Tell them that God is pleased with us when we do our best to learn.

Ask the children to read the banner seven times.

Ask a child to point to the one word that tells what God wants us to do. Give the following study tips:

- Saying things at least seven times helps us to remember.

- Using all five senses to learn helps us to remember.

- Writing down what we want to remember uses touch and sight.

• Saying things aloud uses hearing.

• Sometimes a certain odor such as chocolate can help us remember if we smell it while we are studying. Also, odors of magic markers help us to remember.

• Tracing things with our fingers uses touch. For example, when we study spelling, we can trace the words with our fingers on carpet.

• Repetition helps us to learn. We can put times tables or memory verses on our bathroom mirror so we see and read them often.

Teach today's Bible verse: Ask a child to point to the part of the verse in the banner that tells us what happens when we study hard. Then ask a child to point to the part that tells where the verse is found.

Using a pair of scissors, cut the banner apart word by word and give one piece to each child. Ask the children to put the puzzle together and then read the verse again.

Hand out the printed verses to the children to take home and ask if someone would like to say the verse alone. Allow the children, one at a time, to say the verse without looking as time permits.

Explain to the children that this whole lesson took only ____ minutes and that it really doesn't take much time to learn if we study properly. Include an explanation that God does not expect us all to make A's all the time but that he simply wants us to do our best.

OOOOO

Prayer: Dear Father, please be with us as we study to

please you. Amen.

Parent tip: Prepare a special place for your child to do homework. Establish a routine and have the child do his or her homework at the same time each day. A check-list on the refrigerator listing things the child needs to do is very helpful. The child is responsible for checking off items completed. By doing this, you don't have to keep asking if the child has done his homework. You simply say, "I noticed you haven't finished your homework yet."

September

The lessons this month are geared to help children in their relationships to others. Since this is the first month of the new school year, it is important to get off on the right foot.

Making Friends

Scripture verse: "A friend loves at all times." (Proverbs 18:17)

Materials needed:

• Printed Scripture verses to hand out to children

• Cutout paper fish and write the following on the fish:

- Smile

- Say nice things about others

- Help others

- Don't try to draw attention to yourself

- Include everyone in play

- Pay attention to the needs of others

- Let others go first

- Share

- Don't talk too much

- Listen

• Fishing pole with line and paper clip for hook

• Sheet held up by two people from the congregation or a screen

Procedure: Tell the children that everyone likes to have friends and that today we will be talking about some things that help us to have more friends. Show the fishing pole and tell the children that each one will see if they can catch a fish and that the fish will have a clue for how we can make friends.

Choose the child who is sitting the quietest to be first to use the pole to throw the "hook" over the screen to see if he or she can catch a fish. (Have someone positioned behind the screen to put a fish on the hook in random order.)

One by one, let the children catch a fish and have the group discuss the clue written on the fish with the group.

Introduce the Scripture verse and pass out a copy to each child. Say the verse together several times and explain that the Bible tells us that if we want to have friends, we must be a friend to others.

OOOOO

Prayer: Dear Father, help us to have real love for others and to treat others as we would like to be treated. Amen.

Parent tip: Talk to the children about what some of your friends have meant to you in the past and the things they did that made you love and appreciate them.

Jesus Loves All People

Scripture verse: "Man looks at the outward appearance, but the Lord looks at the heart." (1 Samuel 16:7)

Materials needed:

• A mask or paper bag painted an unusual color such as purple, green, or orange with slits for eyes, nose, and mouth

• A short children's book about a child from another country (May be obtained from your local library or school)

• A small quantity of food from another country or land that is unfamiliar to the children (Many specialty food shops contain foods from other lands.)

• A globe or world map

• Note: Not all of these things are necessary but any or all may be used as available. The main objective is to focus the minds of the children on people who are different in some ways from those being taught.

• Printed copies of the Scripture verse

Questions to introduce the lesson:

Younger children:

• Did God make everyone?

- Did God make you?

- Did God make the people who live far away?

- Did God make everyone to look just the same?

- Did God make the pretty flowers all the same color?

- Did God make all the birds the same color?

- Did God make all people the same color?

Older children:

- As you look around in this group, does everyone look alike?

- Do all of your friends look and act the same?

- How are you like your friends?

- How are you different from your friends?

- Do you choose friends who are like you or different from you?

Procedure: Ask the above questions.

Read and discuss the short children's book. Then put on the mask or colored paper bag. (It would be even more effective if the presenter could actually put on makeup to appear to have a different color of skin.)

Ask the children how they feel about you now that you look different. Ask them if they think you have changed inside because you now have a different color of skin.

Explain that although people may look different and

be different in some ways, we are all of equal value in God's sight. Explain that God looks on the inside of a person to see the heart instead of judging people by how they look on the outside.

Introduce the Bible verse. Say the verse together several times.

Note: Give children a very small sample of the food to eat on their way back to their seats in the church or meeting room.

◯◯◯◯◯

Prayer: "Dear God, help us to love all the people you made and not to judge people by the color of their skin or other differences. Amen."

Parent tip: Make an effort to introduce your children to someone of another race or creed. Point out likenesses. Remind the children that we are to love everyone.

Sharing Isn't Always Easy

Scripture verse: "...whatever you did for the least of these brothers of mine, you did for me." (Matthew 25:40)

• Materials needed: (For this lesson, the presenter should dress in black.)

• Picture of a redheaded woodpecker (Don't forget to check the Internet or some of the computer programs for a picture if another is not readily available.)

• Three loaves of baked bread still in pans hidden in a place where the children cannot see and where the storyteller can get the loaves one at a time (You can buy frozen loaves of dough and simply let them rise and then bake them. In small churches, it may be possible to bake them in the church kitchen and have the odor permeate through the church to give an added effect.)

• A red bandanna or a solid red piece of cloth large enough to use as a scarf on the head

• A white apron

• Printed Scripture verses

Note: This is a lesson based on a story of the redheaded woodpecker. When telling the story, the person in charge should dress in black with the white apron and red bandanna. An older man should be recruited to help with the skit.

Procedure: Explain to the children that a fable is an old story that is not really true but in many cases can teach us real lessons. Tell them that today's story is a fable that teaches us to share.

Role play as you tell the following story:

The Redheaded Woodpecker

Once upon a time, there lived a little old woman who lived all alone in a cabin in the woods. This little old lady always dressed in black, wore a white apron, and tied a red bandanna on her head. [Put on the white apron and red bandanna while speaking.]

This little old lady always baked her own bread. One day, after she had just put a loaf of bread in the oven, she heard a knock on her door. (Old man knocks)

"Who is it?" the little old woman cried.

"I'm just a woodcutter and was passing by and smelled your bread. I am very hungry and wonder if you could give me something to eat," said a voice outside the door.

"Well, come on in," said the old woman. "I just put a loaf of bread in the oven, and I guess I could spare some when it gets done."

The old woodcutter came inside the little house and sat in a chair to wait. By and by, the bread was taken out of the oven.

"Well, I declare," said the woman, "this bread is the prettiest loaf I have ever baked. I'm sorry, old man, but I simply can't share this loaf of bread with you. If you want to wait, I will bake another loaf and you can have some of that."

The old woodcutter patiently waited although he was very hungry. The woman mixed and kneaded another loaf of bread and put it in the oven. All the time, the old man was very hungry.

Finally, the second loaf of bread was done, and the old woman took it out of the oven.

"Well, I can't believe this," the old woman said. "This loaf is prettier than the first. I can't share this pretty loaf with you, old man. If you will wait, I will make another loaf."

Again the old woodcutter patiently waited, all the time growing hungrier and hungrier. Finally the third loaf was done, and the old woman went to take it out of the oven.

"My, my," the old woman said. "This is the prettiest loaf of all. I'm sorry, old man, but you should just go someplace else to get food. I'm not going to share with you. After all, I'm just a poor old woman myself."

At this, the old woodcutter's patience was exhausted. "Because you won't share," he said, "I'm going to turn you into a redheaded woodpecker."

And he did.

Show the picture of the redheaded woodpecker.

Discuss the story with the children. Ask if there have been times when it was difficult for them to share, but they went ahead and shared anyway.

Introduce the Bible verse and have the children repeat it a few times. Tell them that we should be willing to share what we have with others because when we do good things, we are doing good things to Jesus and when we do bad things, we are doing bad things to Jesus.

ооооо

Prayer: Dear Father, help us to share even when it isn't easy. Amen.

Parent tip: Talk with your child about your family belongings and choose something to share with someone else. Discuss the needs of the community or world. Take your child with you when you share.

Respecting the Belongings of Others

Scripture verse: "Thou shalt not steal." (Exodus 20:16, KJV)

Materials needed:

• Printed Scripture verse to hand out to children

• A child's pretty necklace

Procedure: Tell the following story after showing the necklace.

Once upon a time, there was a little girl who came from a poor family who didn't have very many extra things around the house. All of her friends at school seemed to have many pretty things that she wished her mom and dad would buy for her. Every time she would ask her mom for something that was not really absolutely necessary, her mom would look a little sad and say, "Susan, I really wish we could get that for you, but we have only enough money to buy groceries, pay for electricity, and rent. Maybe someday we will be able to get you some pretty things."

One day Susan and her mother were shopping. Susan saw a very pretty necklace and asked her mom if she would get it for her. Again, her mom had a sad look on her face and said, "Susan, we just can't afford it right now. Maybe someday we can get it for you." Susan and her mother were both very sad. Then Susan had an idea.

"Mom," she asked, "what if I work and earn the money and buy it for myself?"

Her mom smiled at her and said, "Susan, you are still young. What could you do to earn some money?"

"I can rake leaves, wash dishes, sweep floors, pick up trash, and pick up black walnuts and sell them," she replied.

After thinking a long time, her mom said, "All right, Susan, if you are willing to earn the money, you may buy the necklace."

Susan was excited. As soon as she got home, she ran to the neighbor's house and asked if they had work she could do. Sure enough, they needed to have their yard raked. Susan worked very hard. She had never raked a yard before and sometimes she had to go back over some places she had raked to do a better job. It was a very warm fall day and she was sweating. Leaves were in her hair, in her clothes, in her nose, and in her mouth. It was not a fun job. Sometimes the wind would blow the leaves back where she had raked, and she would have to do it again. Finally, she heard the neighbor say, "That's good enough, Susan." The neighbor paid her some money, but it was not enough for the necklace.

Susan went to another neighbor's house. "Do you have some work I could do?" she asked.

The lady said, "You know, we just finished our lunch and you may do the dishes if you like."

Susan eagerly went into the kitchen and did the dishes. She did a better job of this than she did raking the leaves because she had more practice. One of her chores at home was to help with the dishes. When she

Pat Lamb

finished, the lady gave her some money.

Susan still did not have enough money for the necklace. She went to still another neighbor and asked if there was work she could do to earn some money. This neighbor liked to mow his leaves but said that there were some sticks in the yard that were too big to mow and she could pick those up.

Susan picked up all the sticks she could find, and when this neighbor paid her, she finally had enough money to buy the necklace!

Susan ran to her mother and shouted, "Mom, Mom, I have enough money for the necklace!"

Her mother smiled and said, "I'm really proud of you, Susan. You have worked very hard. The next time we go to town, you may get the necklace." You see, Susan's mother could not afford the extra gas to make an extra trip to town.

Susan could hardly wait until they went to town again. Finally, payday came, and Susan and her mother went to town to buy groceries. Susan bought her pretty necklace and wore it home! She could hardly wait to take it to school so the other children could see that she had something pretty like they had.

Susan proudly wore her necklace to school. All of the girls commented about how pretty it was. Susan felt so good!

When recess came, Susan decided to take her necklace off so she would not break it while playing outside. She carefully put it in her desk. When the bell rang, she went quickly to her desk to put her necklace back on.

The necklace was gone!

Someone had taken Susan's necklace!

Tears began to well up in Susan's eyes. She looked and looked in her desk, but the necklace was not there. Finally she went to tell her teacher. At first, the teacher thought that Susan had been careless and had just lost it on the playground. She asked the janitor to look on the playground for it. Then she asked the other children if anyone had seen the necklace. No one said that they had seen it.

The necklace was never found. Susan was heartbroken.

Ask the children to tell how they think Susan felt after she had worked so hard and then someone took her necklace. Explain to the children that people's possessions have to be earned. Many people work very hard, and it is wrong to take something that someone else worked for. Include an explanation that no material thing is as valuable as God's love. We should not covet what someone else has. When we start wishing we had what someone else has, then we start being tempted to take that thing.

Introduce the Scripture verse: Ask the children to repeat the Scripture verse and tell them that it is one of the Ten Commandments that God gave to Moses.

OOOOO

Prayer: Dear Father, please forgive us for wanting to take things that do not belong to us. Help us to remember that others have perhaps worked hard for what they have and that we should never steal. Amen

Parent tip: Share stories with your child of a time you lost something you liked very much or when something was taken from you. When they want things, help them understand the cost even to the point of saying, "Dad would have to work _____ hours to pay for that." When a child understands the true cost of things, they respect them more. They need to understand that not only money, but also time and work are involved. Remind them, also, that if we love people, we do not want to do anything to make them feel badly. Taking their belongings would certainly make them feel badly.

October

We're getting ready for winter this month. What better time to emphasize stewardship and planning ahead? We have many examples in nature to illustrate our points. What is the difference between a need and a want? Many children don't know. How does nature relate to our own lives? What must we do to get ready for eternity? All of these thoughts can be tied together in this month's lessons.

Getting Ready for Winter

Scripture verse: "Go to the ant, you sluggard; consider its ways and be wise!" (Proverbs 6:6)

Materials needed: (The following are suggestions. Not all are necessary, but helpful.)

• An ant farm borrowed from a school kindergarten (Ant farms may be available in catalogs of school equipment and supplies. Most elementary teachers receive these catalogs.)

• A small branch from a tree showing attached leaves beginning to turn or pictures of trees beginning to turn

• Any home-canned goods or pictures of the same

• A package of freezer bags

• Printed Scripture verses to give to the children

Procedure: Display the items above. First, using the branch, ask the children what they know from looking at the branch with turning leaves. Winter is coming. The trees will look dead, but in the spring, they will bud again. We know that the weather will change.

Ask the children if they or someone they know has raised any vegetables in a garden or on their patio. Point out that there are seasons when things grow, but they do not grow all the time. Briefly tell about how pioneers had to raise all of their food and had no supermarkets.

Pat Lamb

140

Show the home-canned goods. Ask if any of the children have ever known anyone who canned foods. Explain that at one time, everyone had to find a way to preserve food so they could eat when things did not grow. Show the freezer bags and explain that now many people buy in large quantities to save money and freeze food until it is needed.

Read Proverbs 6:6–11. Discuss with the children that it is important that we plan ahead and be good workers. God will take care of us when we obey him and do the right things, but he doesn't want any of us to be lazy.

Questions for discussion:

• What do we need to do to get ready for winter or times when things may be hard to get? (Save money, take care of what we have, don't waste anything, be thrifty, think ahead to determine needs, and then plan for needs)

• What is the difference between a need and a want? (Ask the children to name needs and then name wants)

• Whose responsibility is it to provide your needs? (Many children will answer "parents." Help the children to see that some of their needs they can take care of for themselves; e.g., sleep, eating properly, making sure they put the proper clothing on.)

Summary: October is the time of year when we get ready for winter. We need to think ahead and decide on needs. Needs should be taken care of before wants. We should not depend upon our parents for everything. We should do what we can for ourselves. God wants us to be good workers.

Introduce the Bible verse: Show the ant farm if one is available. Otherwise, talk about ants and allow the children to tell about ants they have seen. Hand out the printed verses and ask the children to repeat the verse a few times with you.

○○○○○

Prayer: Dear Father, thank you for the many things you have given us. Help us to remember to think ahead and be good workers. Thank you for parents who work to take care of our needs. Amen.

Parent tip: Take time to talk with your children about their material needs. Allow them to join in your planning to help fulfill those needs.

Everything Belongs to God

Scripture verse: "Bring the whole tithe into the storehouse..." (Malachi 3:10)

Materials needed:

• Ten dimes, one dollar bill, ten pennies

• Printed Scripture verses for children to take home

Procedure: In today's lesson, we will introduce the Scripture verse first. Read the verse to the children. Then read the passage, Malachi 3:8–11. Explain that God blesses us when we give one tenth of what we receive back to him. However, he will not bless us if we are doing it just to receive the blessing. He wants us to tithe because we love him and want to do it.

Show the dollar bill and ask how many dimes it takes to make a dollar. Lay them out for the children to see. Take one dime away to show the amount that should be tithed. Have the children count the dimes that are left to see that there are nine and only one went to God's work. More is left than was given. Repeat this process with the dime and pennies. Tell the children that whether we have a little or a lot, one tenth is to be given back to God.

Ask the children where money comes from. Lead them to see that the money comes from work, and there would be no work without the resources God has given us. Therefore, everything comes from God, and everything is really his anyway. Ask, "Do you think God could take the money away from you?" Explain that he wants us to give freely and will not bless us if we are stingy.

Inform the children that God wants us to obey when we are young. We should not wait until we are older to obey God's laws. Good habits are developed early and if tithing is started at a young age, and if done out of love, God will bless that person.

Scripture verse: Repeat the Scripture verse several times together. Tell the children that they may think that their tithe is not very much. The "storehouse" is like a central place to put tithes so that when it is put with other tithes, it becomes a much bigger amount and can accomplish much for the Lord.

ooooo

Prayer: Dear Father, we are sorry for not giving you a tithe in the past. Please help us in the future to remember to give you a tithe. Amen.

Parent tip: When you give money to your child, help the child figure the tenth to give to church or to help someone else. Praise the child for doing so.

Caring for God's Gifts

Scripture verse: "...you have been faithful with a few things, I will put you in charge of many things." (Matthew 25:23)

Materials needed:

- A crumpled bag of potato chips containing only a few chips

- An opened can of soda with a small amount remaining in it

- A crumpled bread bag with a few slices left

- A chart tablet or writing surface

- Printed Scripture verses for children to take home

- Added preparation: Figure the cost of the small amounts remaining in the containers listed above

Procedure: Give the children an opportunity to tell you about a time when they had some money to spend. Allow one or two children to share how they used their money and whether they still have any of that money.

Briefly relate the story of the parable of the talents in Matthew 25. Ask, "What do you think Jesus was trying to teach the people when he told this story?" (Be sure to explain that a talent was a measure of weight.)

Help the children to see that Jesus was trying to teach the people to use their money wisely. We shouldn't "bury" our money, but we shouldn't waste it either. Ask, "Do we ever waste money?" "How do we waste money?"

Using the chart tablet, list the ways the children mention. Include such things as making extra trips to town which uses more gas, taking more food on our plates than we can eat, buying things that are not well made, not caring for our toys or clothing, etc.

Show the items mentioned above. Ask the children if they ever leave pop sitting around that they don't want. Repeat the question concerning the chips. Mention that neither soda nor chips are good for us and that money is wasted to buy them in the first place because they harm us.

Show the bread. Mention that bread can be kept in the freezer for some time, but if we leave it out, it gets moldy. Write the previously figured costs on the chart tablet and add them up to show the children the amount of money wasted. Ask for suggestions of good things to buy with our money and ways to prevent waste.

Introduce the Bible verse: Read the verse and have the children repeat it several times. Explain the verse. Ask if they would like for God to trust them with more, and if so, what they must do.

○○○○○

Prayer: Dear Father, thank you for the many gifts you have given us. We will try to be careful with the things we have. Amen.

Parent tip: When you go shopping, give the child a certain amount of money and require the child be responsible for how it is spent. When they ask you to buy something for them, say, "Is that how you want to spend your money?" or "Do you have enough money?" If they don't have enough money, say, "Maybe if you save your money, you can add it to the amount I give you next time and then you will have enough." This is one way of helping a child learn the value of money and the sacrifice involved in getting wants.

I'll Do My Part

Scripture verse: "If a man will not work, he shall not eat." (2 Thessalonians 3:10)

Materials needed:

• A pretty placemat and a table setting

• Individuals to play the characters in a short skit to act as father and son

• Chart tablet or other writing surface

• Printed Scripture verses for the children to take home

Procedure:

• Discuss with the children how we all enjoy a good meal. Ask if they usually think of the work that has to be done before that meal can be enjoyed. Present the following skit:

Scene: Dad pretends to be cooking in a make-believe kitchen.

Dad: Son, will you please set the table? Your mom will be home from work soon, and we need to have dinner ready.

Son: (Pretends to be busy playing a video game and doesn't answer)

Dad: (A little louder) Son, will you please set the table?

Son: (Continues to play video game)

Dad: (In a much louder voice) Son! I asked you to set the table.

Son: I'm busy, Dad.

Dad: (Goes over to the game and acts as though he is turning it off)

Son: Dad! Why did you do that? That game was fun!

Dad: Son, I know you like to eat. If you want to eat, you must help.

Son: (Begrudgingly) All right! If I have to. But Tommy doesn't have to help at his house. I'm just a kid. Why do I have to do so much?

Discuss the skit with the children. Ask what they think about whether children should help at home. Using the chart tablet, ask the children to tell you ways they are able to help at home. List those ways on the tablet.

Introduce the Bible verse: Hand out the printed verses and ask the children to repeat the verse several times together. Explain that the Apostle Paul wrote this to a church in Thessalonica. This was a rule that had been made for the church there and is an example for us today.

○○○○○

Prayer: Dear Father, thank you for all of the inventions like vacuum cleaners, dusters, and other things that make housework easier. Help me to think of ways to help at home and to be willing to help. Amen.

Parent tip: Discuss with your children the chores they are able to do. As much as possible, allow them to choose their chores. Make a chart to post in an obvious place for children to check off when the chores are done. If there is more than one child in the family, allow them to make their own arrangements with each other to trade if need be. However, make it clear that those chores are their responsibility.

What Do You See?

(Appropriate for Halloween)

Scripture verse: "Man looks on the outward appearance, but God looks on the heart." (1 Samuel 16:7)

Materials needed:

- Printed copies of the Scripture verse to give to children

- Halloween mask

- Sheet

Procedure: Ask the children to discuss their feelings about Halloween. Ask them if they get really frightened, and if so, why.

Have a person who has been contacted ahead of time to come in with a Halloween mask on and a sheet wrapped around him or her. Allow the children to express their feelings. Explain to the children that Halloween began with the Druids and that it was a long time ago. Tell them that now we enjoy the holiday by dressing up and having some fun.

God sees everything, and we don't need to be afraid. Have the person take off the mask and show the person beneath the mask.

Tell the children that things are not always what they appear to be on the outside. Discuss with the children how we often judge people by their appearance but that God always looks at the heart.

Ask a child to tell about his or her best friend. Ask if

they would still like that person if he or she were a different color.

Ask, "What if that person were a different color? What if that person had only one arm? What if that person were not pretty? What if that person had purple polka dots all over his or her body?"

Ask if the children think it changes what people are on the inside by the way they look on the outside.

Tell the children that just as God made flowers and birds in many different colors, he also made people of different colors. God loves us all equally.

Sing: "Jesus Loves the Little Children" with the children, or simply read the words:

> Jesus loves the little children
> All the children of the world
> Red, brown, yellow, black, and white,
> They are precious in his sight.
> Jesus loves the little children of the world.

Scripture verse: Hand out the copies of the Bible verse and ask the children to repeat the verse several times.

○○○○○

Prayer: Dear Father, help me to think of what people are like in their hearts instead of just thinking of what people look like on the outside. Amen.

Parent tip: Use this time of the year when children dress up in costumes to keep reminding them that it is what a person is on the inside that really counts. Be sure to let the children know that we are not really celebrating this holiday, as it had evil beginnings, but that we are just simply having fun dressing up.

November

This is such a busy month! Already, folks are rushing around getting ready for Christmas. It is so easy to skip the important Thanksgiving holiday. Veteran's Day, also, must be given proper attention. We will try to persuade parents to follow through at home so these important holidays will not be neglected.

Being Thankful for My Church

Scripture verse: "I was glad when they said unto me, Let us go into the house of the Lord." (Psalm 122:1, KJV)

Materials needed:

- Copies of today's Bible verse for children to take home

- The church scrapbook if one is available

- If the church has a historian, ask the historian in advance to be prepared to show a few pictures from the scrapbook.

- Pictures of some of the children in Sunday school classrooms

- Pictures, arranged on a large poster, of current church sponsored activities

Procedure: Introduce this month's lessons by discussing the upcoming holidays and their meanings. Allow the children to tell some of the things they are thankful for. Tell them that many people are thankful for the church they attend.

Ask the children to imagine for a moment what things would be like if there were no churches. Help them to understand that church buildings are gathering places where people learn the difference between right and wrong. Although churches can meet in homes or other places, a church building stands as a symbol to the community that people care about worshiping God.

Ask the church historian to show the scrapbook and

tell briefly one interesting thing about the church. (Do not allow too much time to be used here. It is best to tell one or two things and let the children know where the book is kept in case their families want to look at it further.)

Show the pictures on the poster. Of course, it will be most interesting to have included some of the children in the pictures.

Ask the children how they think the church has helped them. Ask all Sunday school teachers in the church to stand and be recognized. Explain that teachers put much time and often much money into preparation to teach because they love God and the children. If it is not possible to have the teachers stand, make plans to provide a way for the children to personally thank a teacher or worker. This might involve one teacher being present in the "big church." If the lesson is being presented at home, the child may make a thank you card for a teacher or worker.

Introduce today's verse: Explain the verse. Ask the children to repeat it together several times.

○○○○○

Prayer: Dear Father, thank you for the many churches and the people who work in them to tell others about you. Help us to show proper respect for the church building and the workers. Amen

Parent tip: Try to think of ways to make going to church a pleasant experience for your children. Prepare clothing the night before to save hustle and bustle on Sunday mornings. You might take children to a favorite place on the way home from church.

Being Thankful for Freedom

Scripture verse: "It is for freedom that Christ has set us free. Stand firm, then, and do not let yourselves be burdened again by a yoke of slavery." (Galatians 5:1)

Materials and preparation:

• Ask a serviceman or woman to come dressed in uniform. If no one is available, ask a veteran to wear his old uniform and come to group time with the children.

• Copies of Scripture verse for children to take home

Procedure: Explain Veteran's Day. Tell the children that you have asked someone who has served in our country's military to come today. Allow the children to ask this person questions. Make sure the following questions are answered:

• Why does our country have military people?

• Why did you join the military?

• What branches of service are there, and why did you choose the one you did?

• What do you do on duty?

• Is your job dangerous?

• Where did you (do you) serve? Is it a long way away?

On behalf of the children, thank the person for his or her service and allow the children to say "thank you" directly. If this lesson is being used in "big church," ask all veterans in the congregation to stand and be recognized.

Introduce today's Bible verse: Hand out copies of the Bible verse for today. Explain that genuine freedom comes when we accept Christ. Freedom is something everyone wants but not everyone has. Sometimes it is necessary to fight to keep our freedom or someone will take it away. Repeat the verse together several times.

○○○○○

Prayer: Dear Father, thank you for our freedom and please help the people in North Korea (or another country you would like to emphasize) to gain freedom so that they may learn more about you. Help us to appreciate those who fought for our freedom and to do the things we can to keep our country free. Amen.

Parent tip: Whenever you see service men or women in public, take a moment to tell them that you appreciate the sacrifices they are making for you. This sets a good example for your children as well as being an encouragement to the servicemen and women.

Why Is This
Happening to Me?

Scripture verse: "And we know that all things work together for good to them that love God, to those who are the called according to his purpose." (Romans 8:28, KJV)

Materials and preparation:

• Research the Internet for information about Squanto and the Pilgrims

• Copies of the Bible verse for children to take home

• A picture of the Mayflower or similar ship

Procedure: Remind the children that our country was founded by a group of people who were seeking a place where they could worship as they felt God wanted them to. When they first came to this country, there were already Indian people here. Many of the Pilgrims died, and they had a very difficult time with disease. If they had all died, history would have been very different.

Many feel that God has blessed our country because the Pilgrims were willing to suffer in order to worship as they felt God wanted them to. Today, the children will hear a story about one person who was involved with the Pilgrims. Ask the children to listen closely and be able to answer some questions after you have finished.

Read the following or tell the story in your own words.

About four hundred years ago, there were some tribes of Indians who lived in what is now Massachusetts. White people did not yet live in this country, but they had been exploring new lands. One time a ship with sails came to the area. [Show the picture of the ship and tell the children that this is the kind of ship that was used at that time.] There were white men from England on the ship. They were exploring the coast. They had never seen Indians before and were fascinated with them. They decided to capture some of them and take them back to England to show people what they looked like. A young boy named "Squanto" was one of the ones captured.

While in England, the men decided to teach Squanto to speak English. When he had learned enough, the man who captured him took him back and used him as an interpreter and a guide. There, he and some other Indian boys were tricked and taken to Spain and sold as slaves. Squanto was recognized and saved after living with some people who taught him about God. He went to live in England and was taken back to America again to be used as a guide for the English. Because he did such a good job, he was allowed to return to his tribe. When he got there, he found that the whole Patuxet tribe had died from a disease! He was the only Patuxet Indian left!

Squanto moved in with another tribe whose chief was Samoset. It was only a short time later that the Pilgrims arrived at Plymouth Rock. The pilgrims were very surprised when they were greeted by an Indian who could speak English!

Squanto moved to the village that the Pilgrims started. He stayed there and taught them to plant, hunt, and fish. He also helped them make treaties with other Indian tribes so they could live peacefully together.

Squanto died in the year 1622. He asked Governor Bradford to pray for him that he might go to the Englishman's God in heaven.

Questions:

• How do you think Squanto and the other Indian boys felt when they were captured?

• How do you think they felt on the ship?

• Do you think it was easy for Squanto to learn English?

• Do you think Squanto ever said to himself, "Why is this happening to me?"

• How do you think Squanto felt when he finally got to go back to his home and all of his tribe had died?

• How do you think the Pilgrims felt when Squanto and Samoset greeted them?

• What would have probably happened to Squanto if he had not been captured?

• What would have happened to the Pilgrims if Squanto had not been captured?

• Do you think that God worked in Squanto's life for a purpose? If so, what was that purpose?

• Do you think you might ever have something

happen to you that you don't understand?

• Do you think God has a purpose for your life?

Introduce the Bible verse: Read the Bible verse together after handing out the printed copies and tell the children what it means. Explain that when we love God and try to do his will, he will work in whatever happens to us to bring good.

OOOOO

Prayer: Dear Father, thank you for Squanto and many other people who allowed God to use them. We know that we are still benefiting from what Squanto did because some of us are descendants from those pilgrims. They started our great country and we are enjoying living here. Amen.

Parent tip: Take your child to the local library and check out some books containing authentic Thanksgiving stories. Don't let this wonderful time be engulfed in Christmas preparations. Take time to help your children appreciate the people who sought to worship God in freedom.

Saying Thanks to God

Scripture verse: "...give thanks to him and praise his name." (Psalm 100:4)

Materials needed:

- A picture of a family sitting at the table
- Chart tablet or writing surface
- Corn, squash, cranberries
- Paper towels or napkins to catch bits of food
- Printed copies of the Scripture verse

Procedure: Briefly review the first Thanksgiving. Tell the children that the pilgrims were so thankful they had survived that they decided to have a feast and invite the Indian people who had helped them.

Show the food items brought. Allow the children to taste the cranberries. Inform them that the Indians called them "ibimi," which means "bitter berry." They were used to treat infections and to make a dye to color blankets and rugs. Mention that many of the traditional foods we serve at Thanksgiving are to help us remember the first Thanksgiving.

Many years later, George Washington, our first president, wrote a letter to Thomas Nelson, Jr., citing how God had intervened in the founding of our nation. He said, "The hand of providence has been so conspicuous in all this, that he must be worse than an infidel that lacks faith, and more than wicked, that has not gratitude enough to acknowledge his obligations."

Much later, Abraham Lincoln wrote a proclamation of Thanksgiving to be celebrated the last Thursday of November. (If time permits, have an older child read the proclamation. A copy can be obtained on the Internet)

Remind the children that Abraham Lincoln said that we have so many blessings that we are prone to forget. Ask the children to try to remember their blessings and list them on the chart tablet. Encourage the children to remember the blessings to say thanks for in their prayers. Suggest that not only should they say thanks to God, but it is also important to say thank you to parents, teachers, and others who do things for us. If this lesson is being used in "big church," ask one or two parents to come to the group. Give their children an opportunity to say thank you to their parents in front of the church. If grandparents are using this lesson at home, encourage and give an opportunity to the children to express their thanks to their parents.

Introduce the Bible verse: Read the verse together several times. Ask the children how they would feel if they worked hard to earn something to give as a gift and then that person didn't even say thanks. God feels badly, too, when we forget to say thanks. Give copies of the verse to the children to take home.

OOOOO

Prayer: (Children will undoubtedly list certain things for the chart as: "I'm thankful for my house, food, parents, church, friends, clothing, and family." Use these items in the prayer for this lesson.)

Dear Father, thank you for my house, food, and family.

We thank you also for friends, clothing, and our church. Amen.

Parent tip: At the Thanksgiving table, go around the table and ask each person to tell what he or she is thankful for. Discuss these blessings. Read a psalm of thanksgiving before the prayer. (The 100th Psalm is appropriate.)

December

Can we really teach children that it is better to give than to receive? We must try! The Christmas season has become so materialistic that we have much competition. The lessons this month emphasize thinking of others. The Christmas story, itself, is usually covered in Sunday school, so we just briefly touch on it here. The other lessons deal with being content, understanding, love, and being kind to others as a gift to Jesus.

Christmas Is a Special Time

Scripture verse: "And she brought forth her firstborn son and wrapped him in swaddling clothes and laid him in a manger; because there was no room for them in the inn." (Luke 2:7, KJV)

Materials needed:

- A doll and long strip of cloth to represent "swaddling clothes" to wrap around the doll

- A picture of a manger

- Printed copies of the Scripture verse

Procedure: Allow a few moments for the children to tell what they like about the Christmas season. Then ask them to explain why we celebrate Christmas. Read or paraphrase the following:

A long, long time before Christ was born, there was a prophet named Isaiah. A prophet is a teacher or someone who told what was going to happen in the future. He told the people that someday a king would be born. He said this about five hundred years before it happened. [Read selected portions of Isaiah 53.]

The people knew that this had been predicted but they did not understand fully. They thought Jesus was going to be a king like a king who sits on a throne. This was not God's plan. Jesus' kingdom covers the whole earth and is made up of those who believe in him. But they knew something special was happening.

Angels appeared to shepherds and told them to go to Bethlehem and see the child.

The shepherds did as they were told. Mary had wrapped Jesus in swaddling clothes. [Demonstrate with the doll and cloth by winding the cloth around and around the doll.] He was lying in a manger. They had tried to find room to stay in the inn, but it was a busy place because so many people had come to be counted for the census.

Jesus didn't have to come to earth. He came as a baby. He was already in heaven with his father, God. He came as a baby and had some of the same problems and temptations we have. He grew up and taught many people how to live. Then he died just as Isaiah had said he would so we could be saved.

We celebrate Christmas because we are happy that Jesus loved us enough to come and show us how to be saved. It is his birthday. We give gifts to each other because the wise men who came later to see Jesus brought gifts. This is a way of showing love to one another, as Jesus wants us to do. We can give a gift to Jesus by obeying him and loving him. Also, we can put money in the offering plate and be kind to others.

Introduce the Bible verse: Read the verse several times together. Show the picture of the manger and explain that it was where the food for animals was placed. Hand out copies of the verse for the children to take home with them.

Prayer: Dear Father, thank you for sending your own son as a baby to grow up and die for us on the cross. We thank you for gifts at Christmas, but we ask you to help us to always remember the real meaning of this special holiday. Amen

Parent tip: Be sure to have a nativity set in a prominent place at home as a reminder to children of the true meaning of Christmas. It is effective to leave Jesus out of the manger until Christmas morning, and then put him in the manger as an indication that he has been born. Do not allow materialistic notions to get in the way of the real meaning of Christmas.

Be Content

Scripture: "Keep your lives free from the love of money and be content with what you have." (Hebrews 13:5)

Materials needed:

- A small inexpensive gift for each child.

- Copies of the Scripture memory verse

Objective: To help the children in developing a concept of the meaning of jealousy and to understand that that feeling is not acceptable to God.

Procedure: Tell the children that today you are going to talk about something that you cannot show a picture of because it is a feeling. Ask the children to see if they can think about what it means to be jealous.

Give a small gift such as a bookmark or some other inexpensive gift to only one child and ask the others how they felt when they didn't get a gift. Tell them that the feeling they felt might be a feeling of jealousy.

Then give a small gift to another child and ask the first child about the feeling experienced. Discuss how many times other people may get something that we don't but that Jesus doesn't want us to be jealous. Explain that Jesus loves all of us equally, but he knows that we don't all need the same things.

Tell the children that God has a plan for each of us and it is different from the plan he has for others.

Read the Scripture verse, and ask the children to repeat the verse with you. Give each child a copy of the verse and then give each child a gift.

OOOOO

Prayer: Father, help us to be happy with whatever is given to us. We realize that many children in the world do not get anything for Christmas. Help me to be happy for what others get as well and not to covet what they have. Amen.

Parent tip: If you have more than one child, talk to your children and tell them that you love them each equally but that it is not always possible to do the same thing for each child. Help them understand that you want to be fair and do as much for one as the other but that needs vary. In your discussion, let the children know that it is your duty as a parent to do your best to meet the needs of each child, but not necessarily to provide wants.

I Love to Give

(Christmas lesson)

Scripture: "It is more blessed to give than to receive." (Acts 20:35)

Materials needed:

• A prettily wrapped box

• Printed memory verses to hand out to children

Procedure: Show the pretty gift box to the children and allow them to unwrap the empty box without telling them that it is empty. When they are surprised to find the box empty, tell the following story.

One time there was a little girl who lived alone with her father. They were very poor. The little girl loved her father very much and wanted to give him a gift for Christmas, but she had no money to buy a gift. The father knew that she had no money and he had none to give to her, so he really didn't expect a gift.

However, on Christmas morning he awakened to find a gift for him. He opened the gift to find nothing in the box. He immediately got angry and asked, "Why did you waste the paper and ribbon to wrap an empty box?"

The little girl looked very sad. She dropped her eyes and then finally got the courage to look at her father. "It isn't empty, Daddy," she said. "I wrapped up my love for you! The box is filled with my love."

Talk with the children about how love cannot always be seen except through our actions. Ask the children to repeat John 3:16, then say only the first part of the verse with them and stop after the word "gave." Tell the children that God loved us so much that he gave. Explain that the wise men brought gifts to the baby Jesus and that the reason we give gifts is to show people that we love them. Emphasize that love is more important than the gift itself.

Talk about the song, "Drummer Boy." If time permits, read the lyrics of the song to them and explain that the little boy in this make-believe story used his talent to give something to Jesus. Ask the children what they can give Jesus to show their love to him. Discuss such things as talking to him in prayer, giving an offering, showing respect in church, obeying his word, and most of all giving him their hearts.

Remind the children that Christmas is a holiday to celebrate the birthday of Jesus and that we should remember to give him a gift for his birthday.

Introduce the Scripture verse: Hand out the Scripture verse and discuss. Allow the children to think and talk a little about whether it is really more blessed to give than to receive. Explain that it is sometimes difficult to understand this verse but hopefully as they grow older they will understand it more fully. Give each child a copy of the verse to take home.

OOOOO

Prayer: Dear Father, We love you and want to give you a gift first. Please show us what we can give you to show our love. Give us wisdom to know what to give others to show our love to them. Amen

Parent tip: As much as possible, allow children to select gifts themselves to give to others. It is better that they give a small gift and have it be something they sacrificed for than to give them money to buy gifts. When you give them money to buy gifts, the gift is really from you, not the child. If need be, allow them to do chores to earn money or help them to make gifts.

A Gift for Jesus

Scripture verse: "…whatever you did for the least of these brothers of mine, you did for me." (Matthew 25:40)

Materials:

- A cup of water

- A slice of bread

- A piece of clothing such as a shirt or coat

- Printed Scripture verses for children to take home

Procedure: Ask the children to share a time when they were very hungry, thirsty, or cold. Ask how they would have felt if there was no place to get food, water, or heat.

Mention that many people in the world do not have all of these comforts. Many people go to bed hungry every night. Some sleep on streets and have no bed. There are homeless people who get very cold sleeping outside. Jesus cares about all people.

Introduce the Bible verse: Show the water, bread, and coat. Ask the children to read the verse together several times. Explain that Jesus is saying that when we are kind to others, it is just like being kind to him. When we are kind to him, that is like giving Jesus a gift. Kindness to others is a gift to Jesus.

Suggest ways that children can show kindness to others. Include the following and allow children to come up with these things themselves, if possible.

Pat Lamb

174

- Say nice things to others.

- If someone drops something, pick it up for him or her.

- Do good deeds for others such as running errands for older people, etc.

- Stay quiet in church so others can hear and not be distracted.

- Pick up trash in church and school.

- Listen carefully when someone is speaking.

- Tell others about Jesus.

- Share your toys, games, pencils, etc.

- Give nice things to others.

- Smile.

- Answer when spoken to.

- Help your parents.

OOOOO

Prayer: Dear Jesus, we love you very much. As a gift to you, we will try to be kind to others and give things to them. Amen.

Parent tip: Set a good example of kindness to others by taking food to a shut-in, etc. Take your child with you to deliver it. Set a good example by staying within budget when gift-giving.

listen|imagine|view|experience

AUDIO BOOK DOWNLOAD INCLUDED WITH THIS BOOK!

In your hands you hold a complete digital entertainment package. Besides purchasing the paper version of this book, this book includes a free download of the audio version of this book. Simply use the code listed below when visiting our website. Once downloaded to your computer, you can listen to the book through your computer's speakers, burn it to an audio CD or save the file to your portable music device (such as Apple's popular iPod) and listen on the go!

How to get your free audio book digital download:

1. Visit www.tatepublishing.com and click on the e|LIVE logo on the home page.
2. Enter the following coupon code:
   97d6-ffbf-23e9-8279-eb05-e325-e424-1736
3. Download the audio book from your e|LIVE digital locker and begin enjoying your new digital entertainment package today!